The Ca
and the Bear

a brief history of the North British Railway

A.J. Mullay

Stenlake Publishing Ltd.

First Published in the United Kingdom, 2016
Stenlake Publishing Limited
54-58 Mill Square, Catrine, KA5 6RD
01290 551122
www.stenlake.co.uk
ISBN 9781840337488

Printed by
Blissetts,
Roslin Road
Acton
W3 8DH

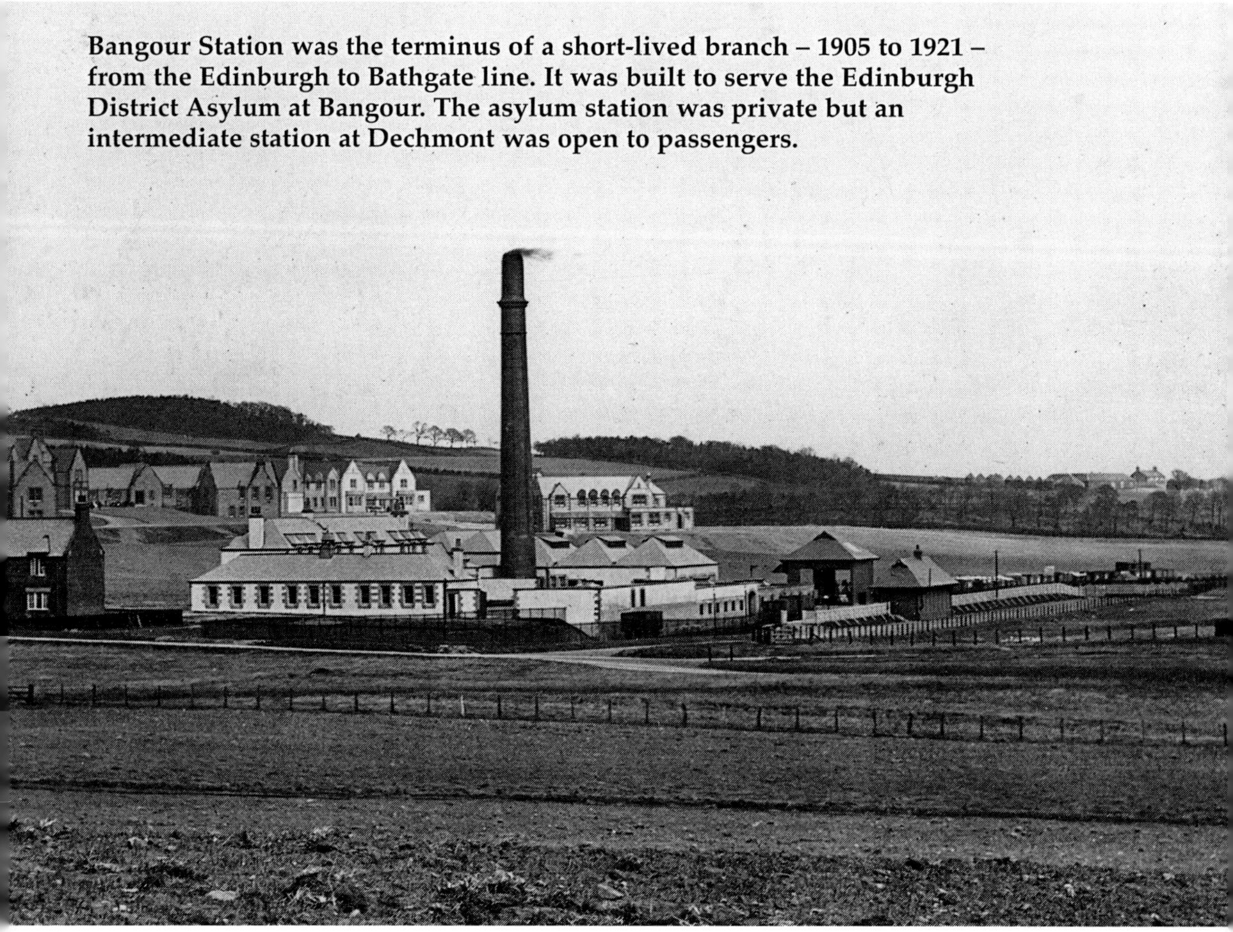

Bangour Station was the terminus of a short-lived branch – 1905 to 1921 – from the Edinburgh to Bathgate line. It was built to serve the Edinburgh District Asylum at Bangour. The asylum station was private but an intermediate station at Dechmont was open to passengers.

Contents

'A Shabby Tiger'	4
Building the Main Line	6
Early Stations	14
North and west	21
Completing the Waverley Route	26
Crossing the Tay – twice	36
Locomotives to 1906	38
Travelling by Night	41
New stations – Edinburgh	43
Burrowing under Glasgow	45
Bridging the Forth	47
Locomotives 1906-22	49
Lothian Lines	53
To the West Highlands	56
Accidents	62
Racing Days	65
Steamers	70
Hotels	72
Docks	75
The End of the North British Railway	76
Chronology	78
Works Consulted	79
Summary of Information	80

'A Shabby Tiger'

That was how the old North British Railway Company was described by historian C. Hamilton Ellis, and it is a comparison worth considering. Although it was the biggest rail company in Scotland, in terms of both route mileage and number of locomotives, the North British lacked the style, indeed the panache, of its rival the Caledonian. Its coat of arms showed simply the castle of Edinburgh and the bear of Berwick-on-Tweed; in contrast, the Caledonian adopted the national arms of Scotland for its insignium. The latter gloried in fast express trains gliding along well-engineered main lines. The North British in contrast, seemed content to muddle along railways which were as difficult to operate as could be imagined. The Waverley Route (Edinburgh-Hawick-Carlisle) and Edinburgh-Dundee-Aberdeen are obvious examples, built piecemeal with sharp curves and challenging gradients clumsily engineered in lieu of expensive earthworks and yet this was the railway which outsmarted the Caledonian to win control of the Edinburgh & Glasgow company and thus gain ownership of Scotland's most important internal route, as well as opening up a huge market in the West of Scotland. It was the NBR which bridged the Tay, not once, but twice, overcoming the effects of a traumatic accident. This company produced Britain's first permanent remote-signalling arrangements, the first British sleeping car, and Scotland's first train-control system. It built the biggest station in the UK in its time, and was a major player in the consortium which built and operated the Forth Bridge, the world's greatest for decades. Its tracks crossed the moss of the Debatable Lands and the bogs of Rannoch Moor. Its uniquely-liveried locomotives were seen in Mallaig, Aberdeen, deep under the city of Glasgow, and only yards from the shore of Loch Ness. It may have been shabby, but, like most tigers, it was not a company to mess with.

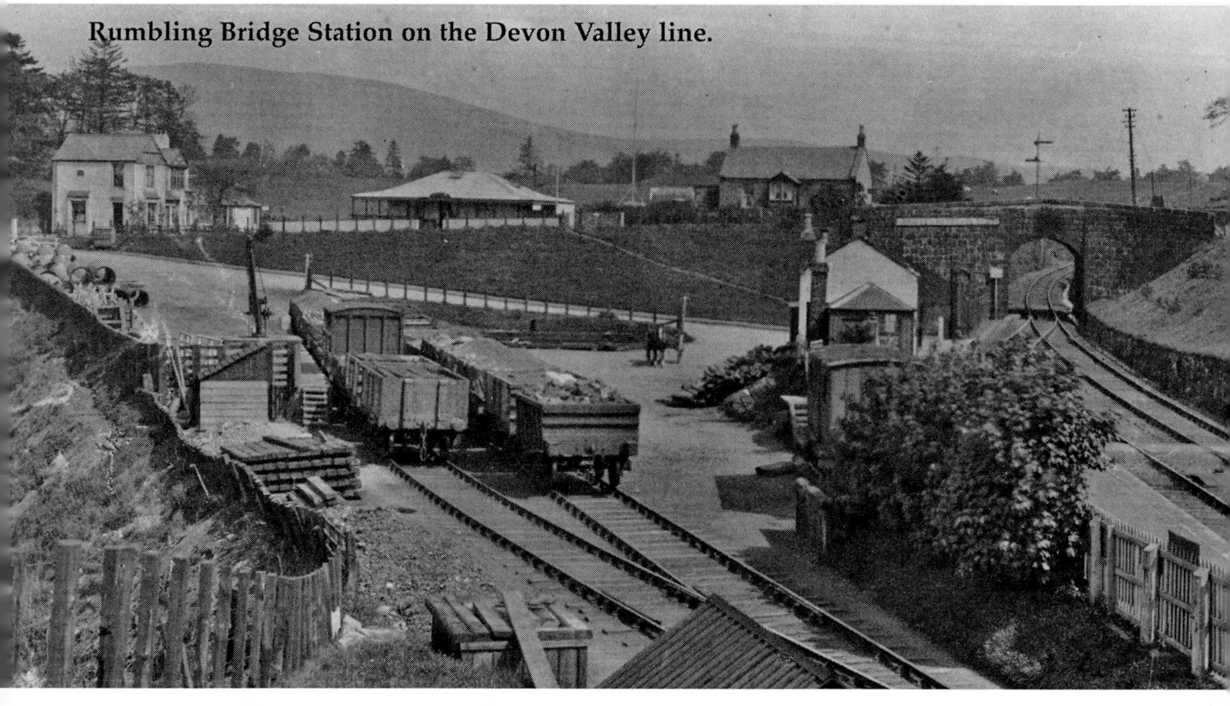

Rumbling Bridge Station on the Devon Valley line.

NBR Network

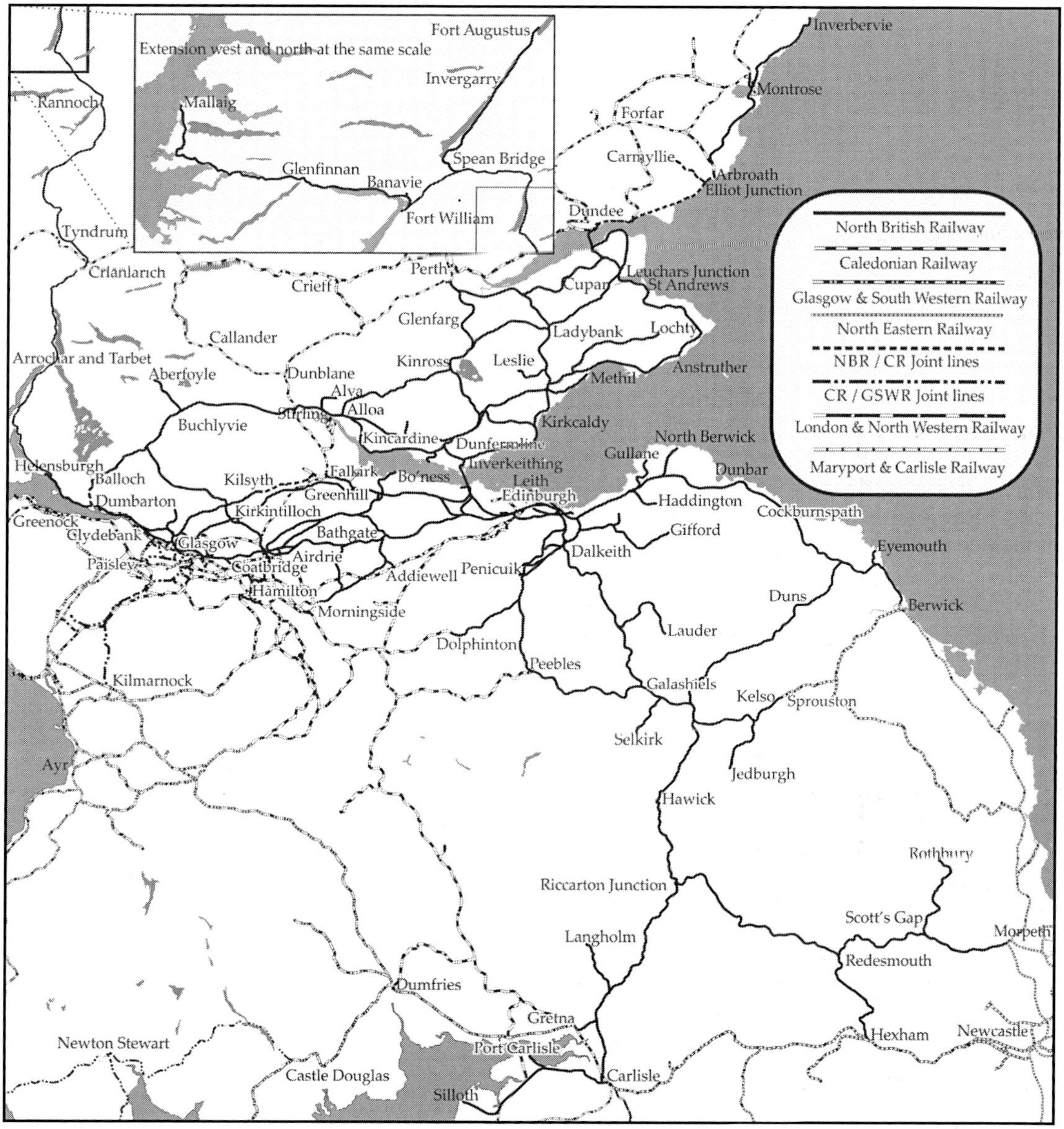
Extension west and north at the same scale
Fort Augustus
Invergarry
Mallaig
Spean Bridge
Glenfinnan
Banavie
Fort William
Inverbervie
Montrose
Forfar
Carmyllie
Arbroath
Elliot Junction
Dundee
Rannoch
Tyndrum
Crianlarich
Perth
Crieff
Leuchars Junction
St Andrews
Cupar
Glenfarg
Ladybank
Lochty
Callander
Kinross
Leslie
Anstruther
Methil
Arrochar and Tarbet
Aberfoyle
Dunblane
Alva
Alloa
Stirling
Buchlyvie
Kincardine
Kirkcaldy
Dunfermline
North Berwick
Gullane
Inverkeithing
Helensburgh
Balloch
Falkirk
Bo'ness
Leith
Dunbar
Kilsyth
Dumbarton
Greenhill
Edinburgh
Haddington
Kirkintilloch
Cockburnspath
Greenock
Clydebank
Glasgow
Bathgate
Gifford
Paisley
Airdrie
Coatbridge
Dalkeith
Eyemouth
Addiewell
Penicuik
Hamilton
Duns
Berwick
Morningside
Lauder
Dolphinton
Peebles
Kilmarnock
Galashiels
Kelso
Sprouston
Selkirk
Ayr
Jedburgh
Hawick
Rothbury
Riccarton Junction
Scott's Gap
Morpeth
Langholm
Redesmouth
Dumfries
Gretna
Hexham
Newcastle
Newton Stewart
Port Carlisle
Castle Douglas
Carlisle
Silloth
North British Railway
Caledonian Railway
Glasgow & South Western Railway
North Eastern Railway
NBR / CR Joint lines
CR / GSWR Joint lines
London & North Western Railway
Maryport & Carlisle Railway

Building the Main Line

Unlike its greatest rival, the North British Railway was founded on Scottish fortunes. While dependent on an English partner company to complete an east coast route between the capital cities of England and Scotland, it was master of its own destiny, an Edinburgh company managed, largely, by Edinburgh men. In contrast, the Caledonian, was dominated by English interests. Ironically – in view of its name, with the implied emphasis on the *the* – the "Caley" was floated with 77% of its funding from English shareholders. Comparing the two prospectuses, the NBR's printed in Edinburgh and the CR's at Westminster, the NBR's capital was £900,000 and the CR's exactly double. Share prices were £25 and £50 respectively.

The map illustrated on the back of the NBR prospectus of 1843 shows a main line extending south from Berwick and Newcastle, passing west of Darlington, and then reaching London via Sheffield and Rugby. The first two names shown on the provisional committee were the lord provost of Edinburgh and the mayor of Berwick-upon-Tweed. This 'homely' quality was to serve the company well. In contrast, the Caledonian's English support base proved to be a massive disadvantage as soon as the feeblest of recessionary winds began to blow in the late 1840s and the company's masters found that funding requests made to its supporters fell on deaf ears. After all, the proponents of a west coast main line had to see the grand junction finished and the Lakeland fells conquered before they could start even thinking about forging northwards from Carlisle across the rivers of the Debatable Lands and addressing the foothills of the Lowthers.

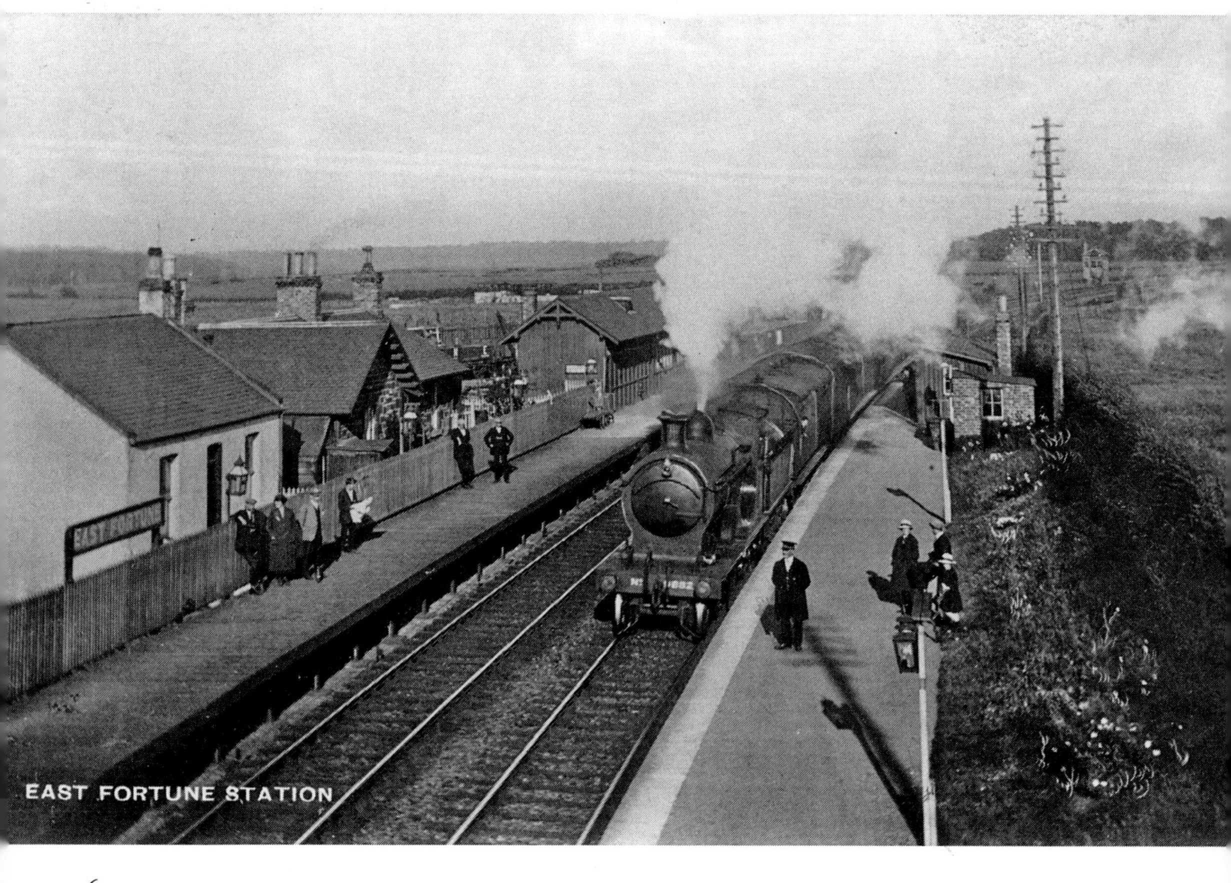
EAST FORTUNE STATION

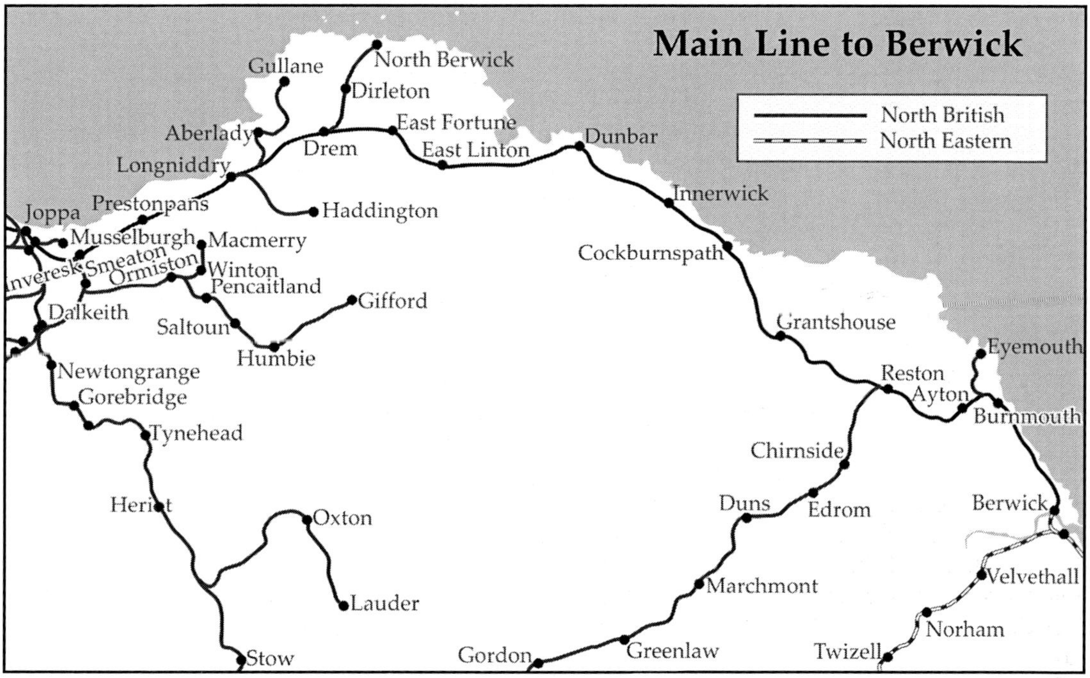

This meant that the favour bestowed on the Caledonian by the government's Smith-Barlow Commission, which in 1841 recommended one central rail route between England and Scotland (effectively the Caledonian line) – was qualified by a provision for other routes to begin construction if the Caledonian line was delayed, and it was. While dependent on an English partner company to complete an east coast route between the capital cities of England and Scotland, the NBR was financially independent and free to begin constructing its main line as soon as it wished. The company's directors may have had more limited ideas than their Caledonian rivals initially, but they were able to build southwards quickly, and rapidly grew in confidence as the "Railway Mania" flourished in the mid-1840s. Although the municipal crests of Edinburgh and Berwick-on-Tweed (a maiden and hind supporting a castle, and a bear chained to a tree, respectively, surrounded by thistle and rose) were the only ones displayed on the insignium of the North British Railway (and were to retain this unique status) the company's directors were looking further afield from the start.

A route to Hawick became a possibility from the outset, with their 1845 purchase of the Edinburgh & Dalkeith Railway. This was made initially to gain access to the all-important port of Leith as well as to remove a rival opposing the NBR's incorporation, but it also availed an immediate opportunity to penetrate south from the city into the productive Midlothian coalfield, then south to Hawick. A possible second route to England beckoned, one not incumbent on the NBR maintaining good relations with "Railway King" George Hudson. Of course, this was fairly typical of boardroom attitudes in the mid-1840s – planning a second main line to England before the first was anywhere near complete! In fact, the 58 mile line to Berwick posed many problems for the inexperienced NBR directors. They chose badly when it came to appointing a contractor for the Cockburnspath section and a riot was reported there in October 1845, almost certainly because the unfortunate navvies (from 'navigators', the men who had cut the canals to create a major transport network all over Britain in the previous 70 years) were victims of the 'truck' system already outlawed in industry. Under this arrangement, the workers received their pay in credit notes realisable only in shops provided by the employing contractor, and poor quality food and beer was the usual fare supplied. In true Victorian style, the grievances were dealt with punitively – the NBR records showing that the company paid for the hire of more constables by the local authorities concerned, and hesitating not one moment to pay extra for handcuffs and truncheons. It might have been cheaper to have ordered the contractor to sell better beer!

The directors toured the line, or what existed of it, in the autumn of 1845, and could not help noticing that the Houndwood section, let to a more enlightened contractor, was far in advance of the Cockburnspath section to the north. Here the directors informed their board that the workers "looked as if they were emerging from a state of mutiny, sullen and discontented". Unfortunately for the company, its directors had followed the contemporary habit of offering shares in the railway to the contractors in partial payment. This of course meant that the contractor could hardly be sacked!

One unfortunate action which the board authorised was the almost complete demolition of Berwick Castle, despite the protest of (only) two local residents, the Misses Askew. Was this some act of revenge by the Scots for the loss of Berwick-on-Tweed to the English in the 15th century? Certainly, the NBR directors had no intention of building south from Berwick as it was understood that the partner English company (the Newcastle and Berwick Railway) would bridge the Tweed. Just to compound the historical sacrilege which the NBR committed at Berwick, the company spared all possible expense in giving the town its station. Berwick may have been good enough to feature with Edinburgh on the NBR badge – and no other community was so honoured, no matter how big the company became – but Berwick Station was a disgrace. According to O.S. Nock, "it was built in masonry largely recovered from the demolition of the castle ... but the foundations were unsound". Nock believes that it nearly collapsed within a year of construction, but whether this is exaggerated or not, the fact is that a 5 mph speed restriction was necessary through what *The Times* called the "squalid platforms" until the LNER took the place in hand in the 1920s, building the island platform which exists to this day.

The first train to run between the Scottish capital and the Border left the North Bridge station in two sections on 18th June 1846. The first consisted of twelve coaches – their number doubled at Dunbar – with no fewer than four locomotives powering the train up Cockburnspath Bank. The second train consisted of five engines powering 26 coaches! A sumptuous dinner was served to the 700 invited travellers at Dunbar on the return journey, and the company could relish the fact that they had well and truly defeated the Caledonian, supposedly the 'official' railway to connect Scotland and England. Unfortunately, the day did not end in triumph, a railwayman being killed at Longniddry on the return journey, apparently adjusting oil lighting on the roof of one of the trains while in motion. The company papers do not appear to record any compensation being paid to his family. This is still the principal railway line between the English and Scottish capital cities. Some changes have been made in Berwickshire – the line has been moved back from the cliff edge near the actual Anglo-Scottish Border at Lamberton, and Penmanshiel Tunnel has been bypassed following an accident there in 1978. Otherwise, it remains largely as built by the North British Railway Company more than 150 years ago, although the permanent way is different in detail.While the original NBR track comprised 70 lb rail laid in lengths of no more than sixteen feet, nowadays heavy high tensile steel rail is welded into almost endless lengths. It is the route of the 'Flying Scotsman' train, first

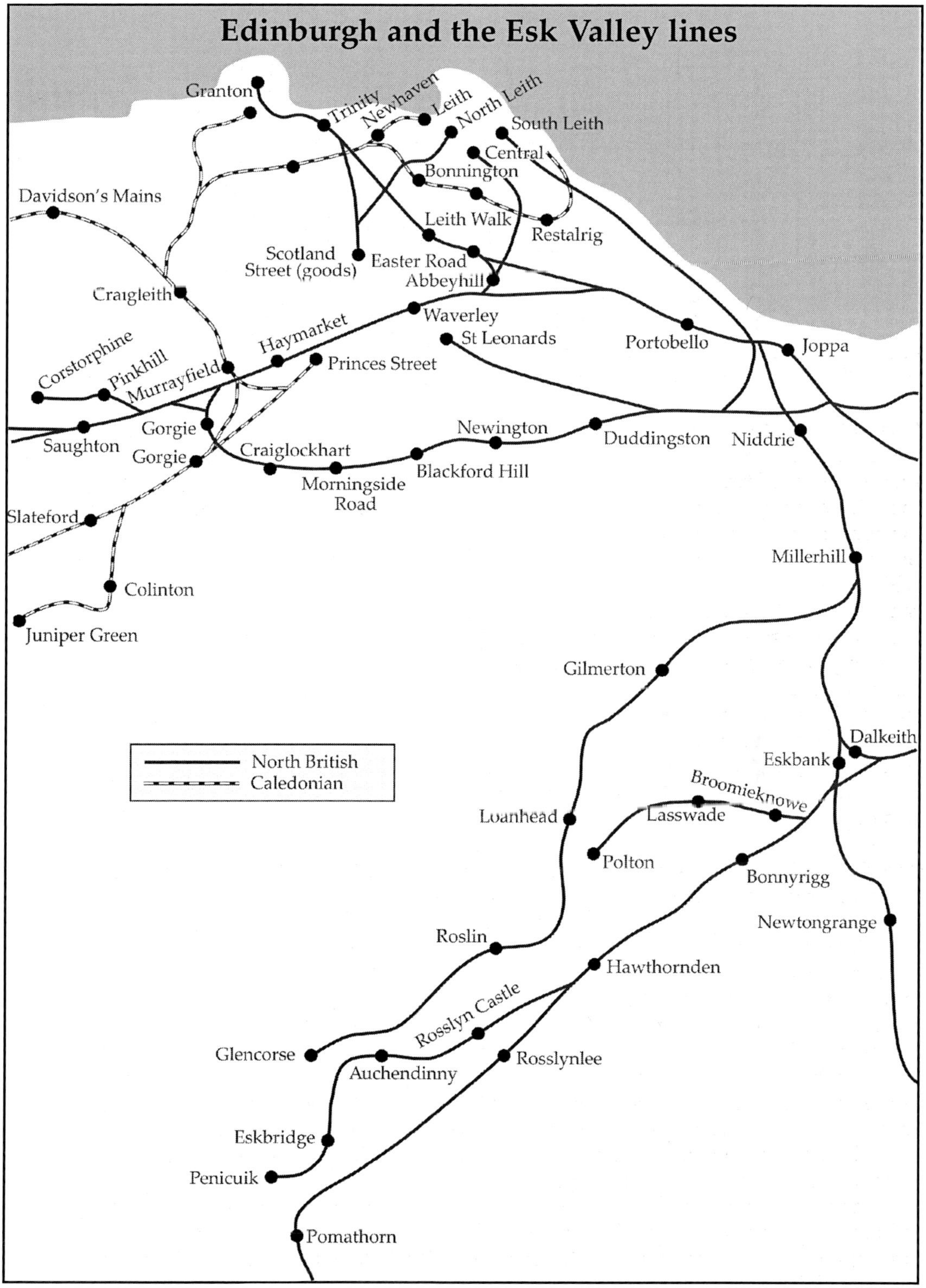

Edinburgh and the Esk Valley lines
Granton
Trinity
Newhaven
Leith
North Leith
South Leith
Central
Bonnington
Davidson's Mains
Leith Walk
Restalrig
Scotland Street (goods)
Easter Road
Abbeyhill
Craigleith
Waverley
St Leonards
Portobello
Joppa
Corstorphine
Pinkhill
Haymarket
Murrayfield
Princes Street
Saughton
Gorgie
Gorgie
Craiglockhart
Morningside Road
Newington
Blackford Hill
Duddingston
Niddrie
Slateford
Colinton
Juniper Green
Millerhill
Gilmerton
North British
Caledonian
Dalkeith
Eskbank
Broomieknowe
Lasswade
Loanhead
Polton
Bonnyrigg
Newtongrange
Roslin
Hawthornden
Rosslyn Castle
Glencorse
Auchendinny
Rosslynlee
Eskbridge
Penicuik
Pomathorn

Ayton Station

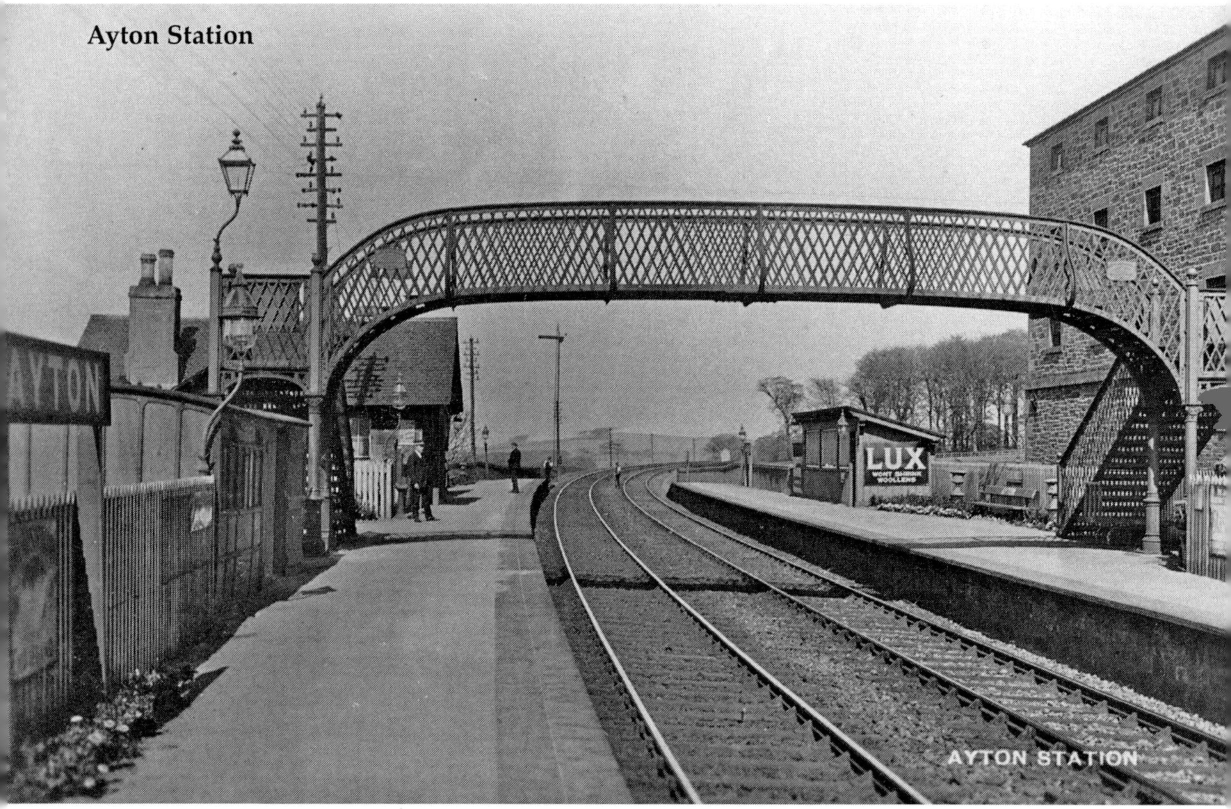

operated back in 1862, and has carried the longest non-stop runs regularly scheduled anywhere in the world. Its track has seen the frenzied passing of the racing trains of 1888 and 1895, the streamlined *Coronation* in the late 1930s, and the sedate *Queen of Scots* Pullman in the 1950s. It has conveyed Aberdeen fish, Lothian coals, and, nowadays, nuclear spent fuel. At the present time it carries trains operated by two private companies. Imagine if today's privatised companies had been required to build a railway line as well as operate it! That is the measure of what the old North British Railway achieved – and with no public handouts!

One of the North British Railway's problems at the end of 1845 was that the Caledonian Railway shareholders, who had yet to lay a yard of track, were avariciously announcing extensions and branches to any town they could find on a Scottish map! A good example was Peebles, which in February 1846 was the ridiculous object of a treaty between the two companies. The Caledonian graciously consented not to build lines east of Peebles, if the North British agreed not to construct a (hastily-planned and announced) line from Peebles to Biggar. Yet the NBR was not yet within 20 miles of Peebles (indeed, that town's first railway was staunchly independent of the NBR to begin with), while the Caledonian had never turned a wheel. No wonder this period is known as the 'Railway Mania'!

Just as the Caledonian gained access to Glasgow by negotiating running powers over two mineral railways, so the North British found it highly convenient to secure ownership of the Edinburgh & Dalkeith Railway. Described by contemporary historian Robert Chambers as the "Innocent Railway", the Edinburgh & Dalkeith Railway holds an important place in the development of Scottish transport. Before the NBR had so much as turned a wheel, the older company was bringing coal trains through a tunnel under Sampson's Ribs (in Edinburgh's Queen's Park) into the city's first rail terminus at St. Leonard's. It also owned the first station in Leith, running there from Seafield and Portobello on a line which is still used today by freight trains. It was highly effective in its coal-carrying role, St. Leonard's being the railhead for most of the city's south side until well into the 1960s, something which would have pleased its aristocratic backers, all of them owners of Lothian mines. Historian C.J.A. Robertson enumerated them as 'a duke, a marquis, two earls, a viscount, and five baronets' – not bad for a horse-drawn waggonway! The railway also operated passenger services, although with some difficulty if Chambers is to be believed, with early travellers refusing to state their destination to 'ony speirin' loon' of a ticket collector!

The significance of the North British takeover of the Edinburgh & Dalkeith Railway was threefold. Firstly, it removed an objector from among those opposing the NBR's construction in the Portobello area. Secondly, it provided an immediately available route to Leith, then one of Scotland's most important ports. Thirdly, it provided an arm of railway reaching south into the Lothian coalfield, but also towards the first range of Border Hills and towards England.

The NBR directors were perfectly prepared to build a second main line southwards before the Berwick line was complete. In 1844, they commissioned John Miller (engineer of the

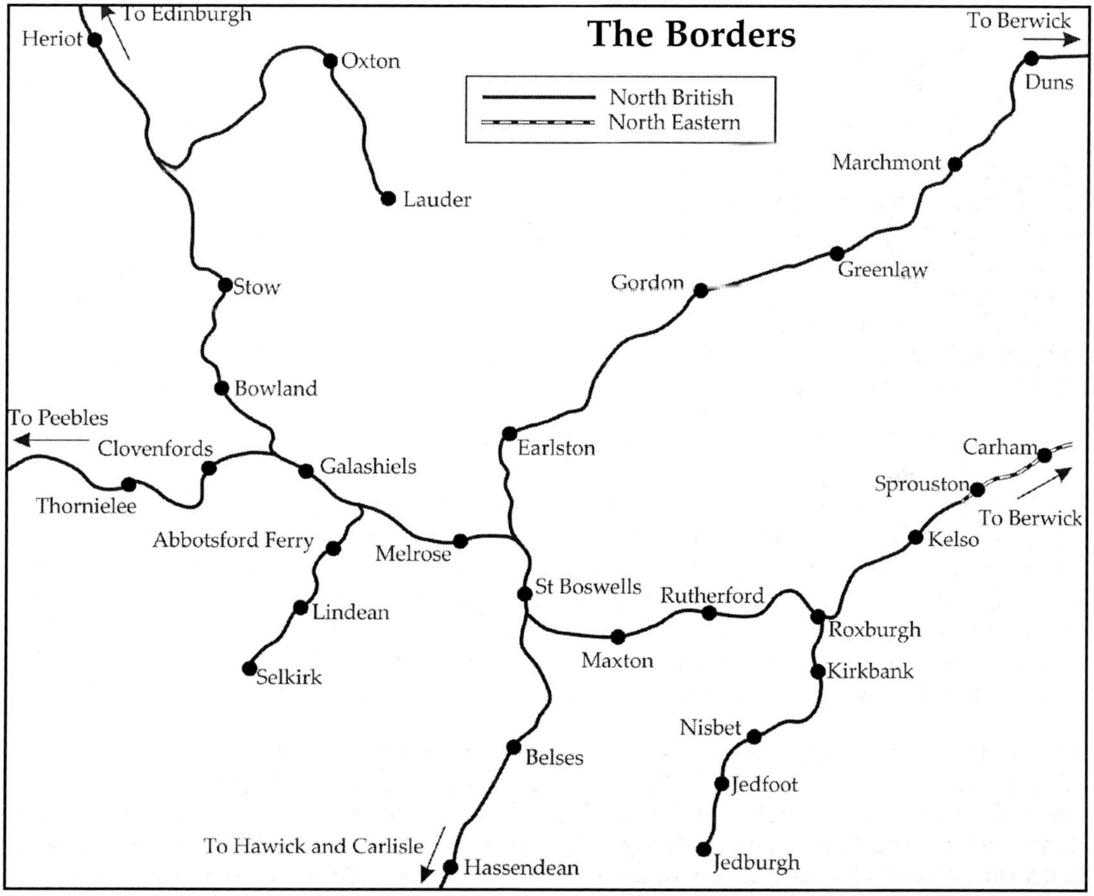

Edinburgh-Glasgow line) to investigate a line as far south as Hawick, including a branch along the Tweed to Kelso. This was not impracticable; by purchasing the Edinburgh & Dalkeith Railway, the NBR was already at Newtongrange, and work was soon under way to tackle the climb into the Moorfoot Hills. Like all capital projects, it seems, the Hawick branch was costed inadequately, with the shareholders being told that no major earthworks would be required. Quite how the 1,000 feet high Falahill Pass was to be crossed without earthworks was not made clear! The spectacle of a line south from Hawick to the English border was quite enough to encourage the NBR to forge southwards. Borthwick Embankment, south of Gorebridge, soon required such earthworks as to render the company's earlier costings as fictional, and even when Falahill had been crossed, the Gala Water required no fewer than seven bridges north of Galashiels, while south of there a major bridge was required over the Tweed. Hawick was not reached until November 1849, the original station being aligned to allow for a possible route along the west bank of the Teviot and thence southwards to Mosspaul Pass. This is the route which the A7 takes, and is the obvious path for any railway to follow from Hawick to Carlisle. However, no railway connecting these communities would be complete until two decades later, and Mosspaul has never seen a railway.

The Hawick Branch, which became the basis of the 'Waverley Route', was far more expensive to build per mile than the East Coast line to Berwick, and offered no foreseeable promise of English traffic. Indeed, so expensive was it, soaking up all the

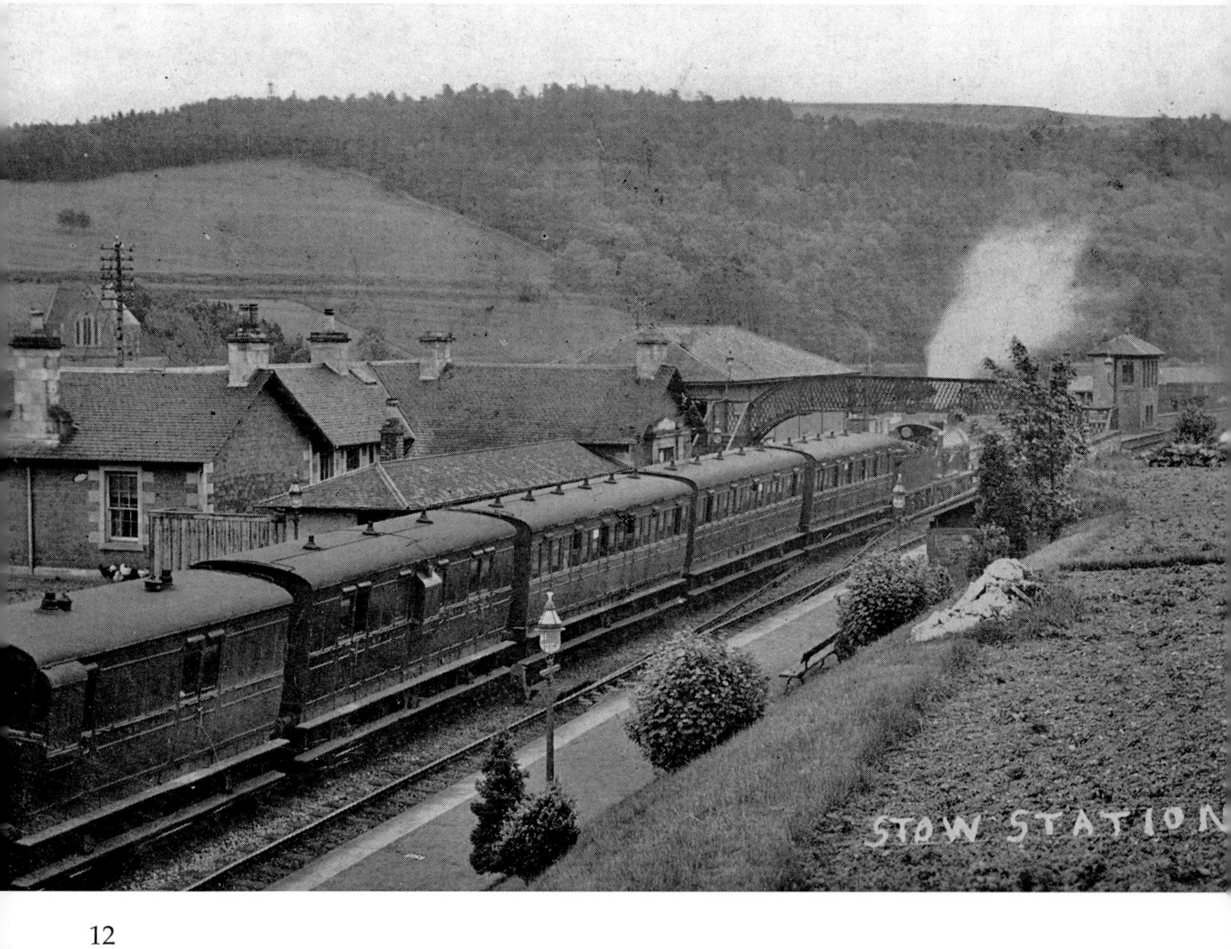

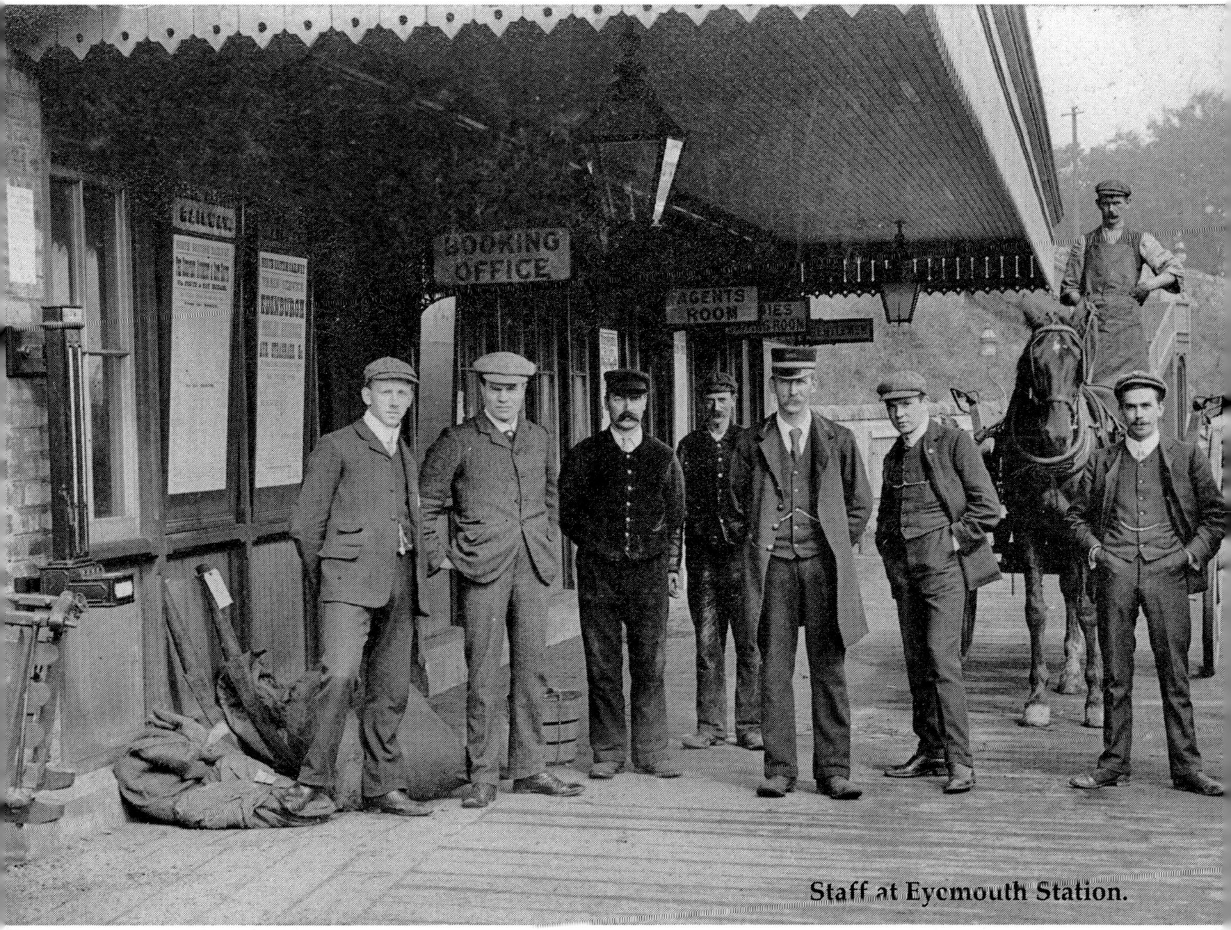

Staff at Eyemouth Station.

turnover of the Berwick line, that by the end of 1848, the NBR had to go cap in hand to the York, Newcastle and Berwick Railway, seeking amalgamation, or offering a lease on the Edinburgh-Berwick line. While this did not materialise, the situation was hardly eased when the branch was fully open. Fifteen years later, shareholders were told officially that "nearly one half of the NBR system, instead of being remunerative to the company, must operate as a drawback on the profits of the remainder". No prizes for guessing that the problem lay with the operation of an expensively built branch line to a burgh where one of the townspeople has been heard to remark "A day out of Hawick is a day wasted!" Perhaps some market research might have been carried out beforehand – but such a concept was unknown to the Victorians. In particular, it seems unfortunate that the NBR directors, having aimed realistically and successfully at opening a 56-mile main line into northeast England, failed to use their remaining capital and accumulated experience to more immediately profitable ends. A start could have been made in crossing the Tweed, turning the Royal Border Bridge into a joint structure, thus giving the Edinburgh company a much stronger hand in its subsequent dealings with the North Eastern Railway coming up from the south.

With the NBR newly, and expensively, linking Edinburgh with Berwick and Hawick by the halfway point of the 19th century, it is time to return to the capital, and examine the beginnings of Waverley Station – the most important in the system.

Early Stations

Charles Darwin, a student in Edinburgh in September 1825, peered over the city's North Bridge expecting to see "a fine river". Instead, he glimpsed a bustling market far below. By a strange coincidence, just as the 19th century's greatest scientific thinker was viewing this Edinburgh site, nearly 200 miles away to the south, another great product of that century, the public railway had just made its appearance.

The Edinburgh descendant of the Stockton and Darlington did not find its way under the arch of the North Bridge until some 21 years later. In 1846 the North British Railway decided to make this site its city centre base, and its suitability was perhaps questionable. The remaining market site had to be compressed into the land spanned by the middle and southern arch, a replacement site not being provided for many years, indeed decades. More damagingly, Trinity Church had to be dismantled (for sidings!) with pioneering conservationist Lord Cockburn describing this as "an outrage by sordid traders, virtually consented to by a tasteless city and sanctioned by an insensible parliament". He also campaigned against what appeared to be an operational corollary – the extension of the

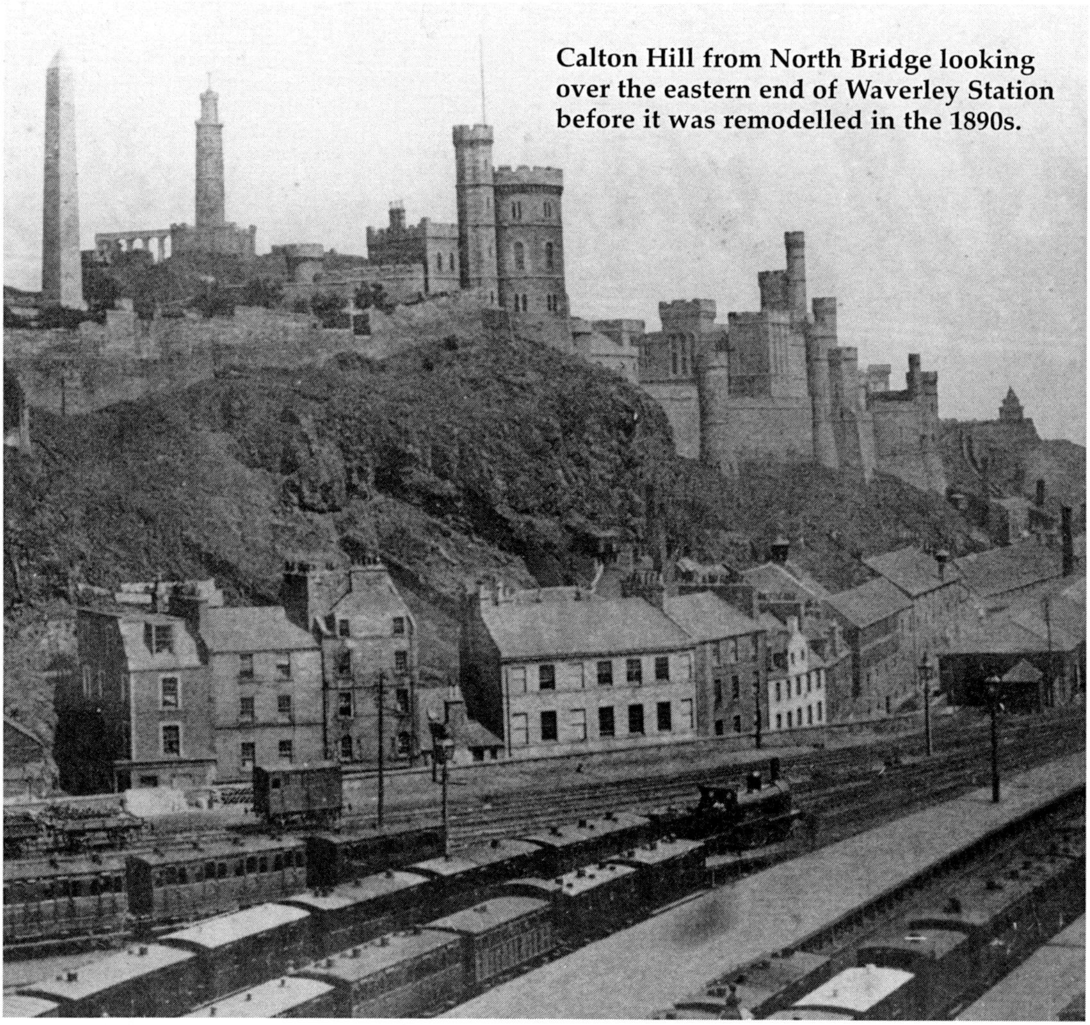

Calton Hill from North Bridge looking over the eastern end of Waverley Station before it was remodelled in the 1890s.

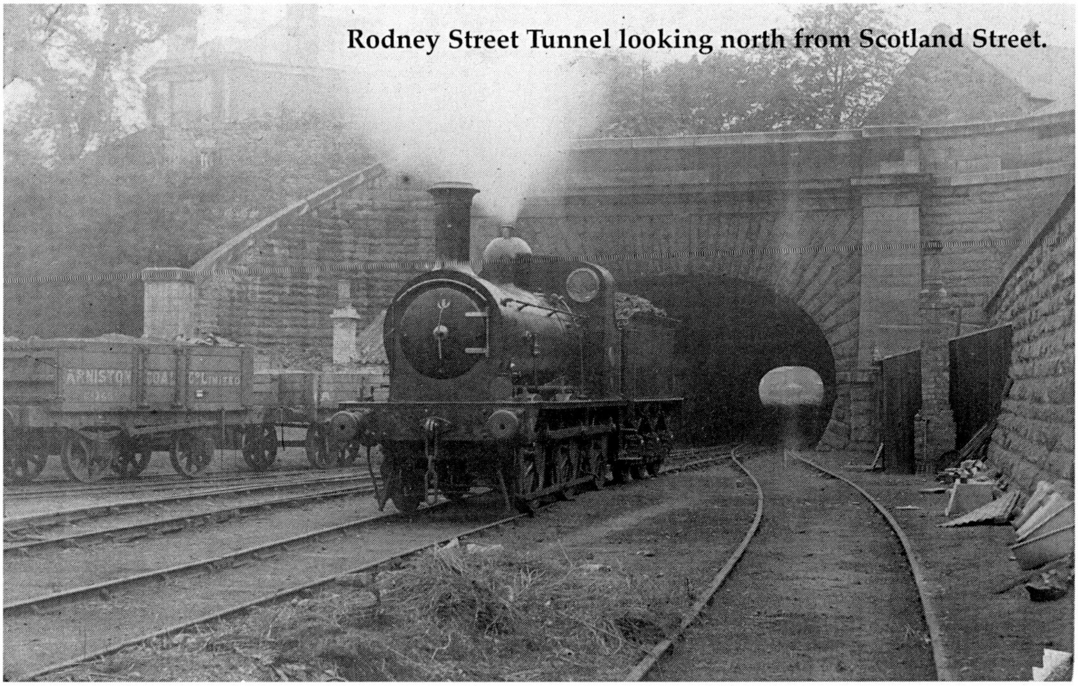

Rodney Street Tunnel looking north from Scotland Street.

Edinburgh and Glasgow Railway through Princes Street Gardens from its 1842 eastern terminus at Haymarket, not that this must have worried the NBR directors in the mid-1840s. The destroyers of Berwick Castle proceeded to dismantle Trinity Church, laying their rails under the North Bridge, and then building a train shed connecting by stairs with Waverley Bridge, where the ticket office (now a fashionable eating-place) was to be found. Not only did trains leave this location to east and west – but also northwards! In the northwest corner of the site, (not yet called Waverley; the NBR board minutes call it 'Edinburgh Station') was another station entirely. Although separated from the main station by a now-vanished thoroughfare called Canal Street, from which it took its name, there was rail connection to the Edinburgh & Glasgow Railway almost beneath the Scott Monument. This northbound line was constructed by the Edinburgh & Northern Railway, which operated trains down a rope-worked incline in tunnel to Scotland Street, where a steam locomotive would take Dundee or Aberdeen passengers on to Granton to their next endurance test, the ferry to Burntisland.

Until 1868, the Scotland Street tunnel was an integral link between the Waverley site and the northern cities, until the NBR managed to take over the parent company – another famed for the incompetence of its directors – and constructed an alternative line through Abbeyhill, Easter Road, Leith Walk and Powderhall, joining the Scotland Street – Granton line at Trinity. Scotland Street remained as a passenger terminus for a surprisingly long period, for trains to and from Granton, but the incline was abandoned. The tunnel is still there, commandeered as a control centre during the Second World War, and leased at different times to commercial interests for mushroom-growing and car storage.

Taking over the line meant that the NBR now had a second passenger terminus in Leith – it was already in South Leith, thanks to its takeover of the Edinburgh & Dalkeith Railway, but its new Citadel terminus (later North Leith) also allowed direct access to Leith Docks across Commercial Street. The Granton passage was already served by roll-on, roll-off ferries using

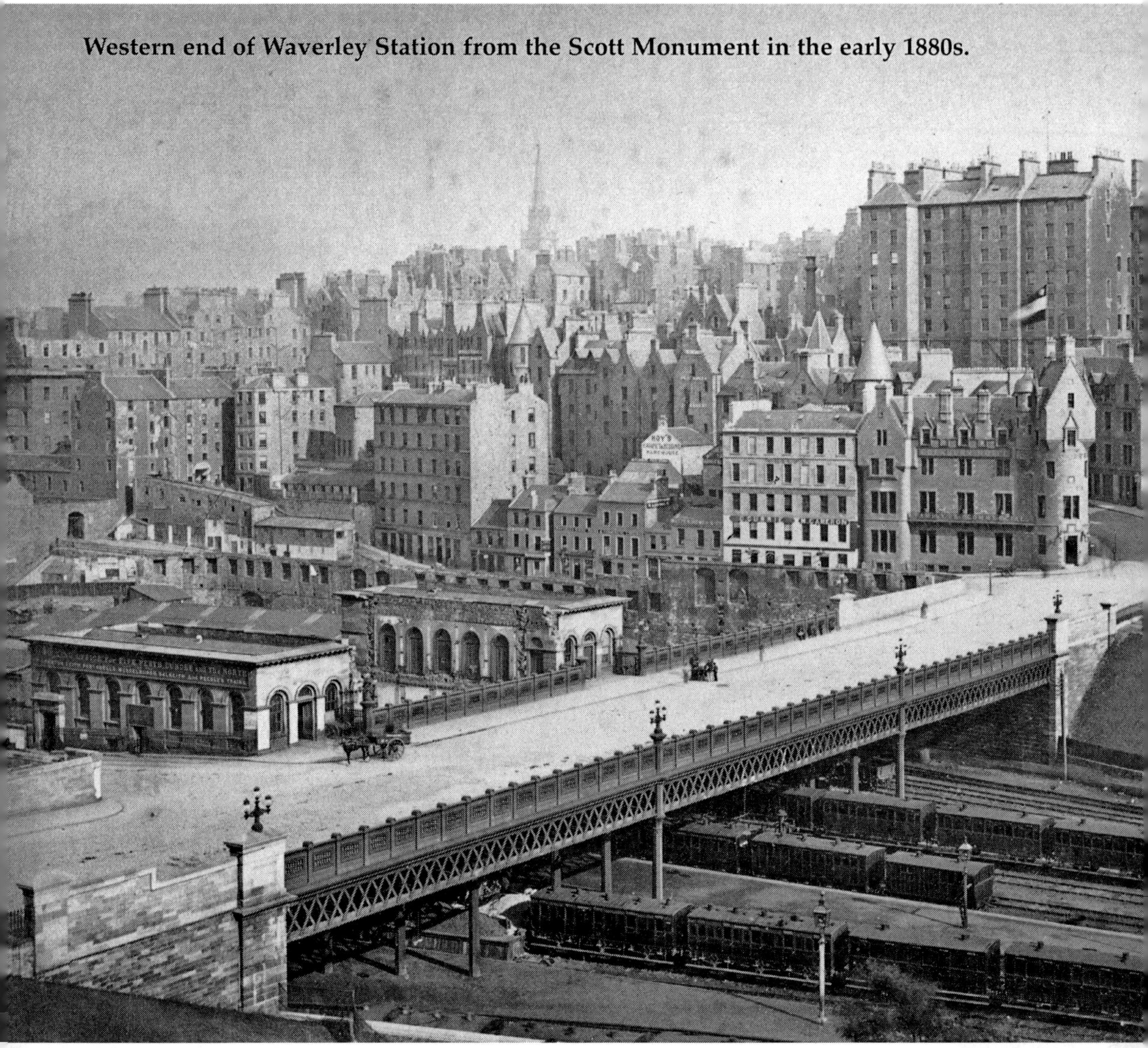

Western end of Waverley Station from the Scott Monument in the early 1880s.

a loading (rail) ramp designed by Sir Thomas Bouch, which appears to have been one of his more successful works.

So busy had the (newly-named) Waverley Station become by the 1860s, that it was becoming almost impossible to rebuild and extend, since so much disruption would be caused. As well as running trains eastwards to Berwick and Hawick, there were ferry trains to be run to Granton for the Fife, Dundee, and Perth traffic. With the opening of the Abbeyhill line in 1868, these would start from the main line platforms at Waverley, with the northbound platform catering for both arrivals and departures within its length. Glasgow and Larbert trains used the southern platform, but already the company was having to use up space on the northeast and south sides, among the goods lines, to improvise extra platforms to cater for suburban traffic. The Caledonian even ran into Waverley, sharing Edinburgh-Stirling traffic (in truth, its own city terminus was little better than Waverley). While the idea of configuring Waverley as a through station was a good one, its capacity was severely inadequate for its new services as the NBR became one of Scotland's leading transport utilities. Unfortunately, this was to remain unchanged until the late 1880s.

Meanwhile Haymarket had changed from a terminus to a through station. Built in 1842 by the Edinburgh & Glasgow Railway as the original company terminus in the capital, Haymarket boasted a fine façade looking almost eastwards to Princes Street, although stone-cleaning was required to reveal the finer points of the building. The original train shed below, with its cast iron columns and elliptical arches, became redundant with the boring of the tunnel to Princes Street Gardens in the 1840s (the second bore was completed some 40 years later) and the shed can now be found lovingly preserved on the Bo'ness and Kinneil Railway.

Almost rivalling Waverley in size, and excelling it in awkwardness to operate, Glasgow's Queen Street Station entered the NBR assets ledger in 1865. Although only a few yards from the city's George Square, the station suffered from being built at a much lower level than the company intended. Forced by canal interests to drop their line 150 feet in only 1½ miles, the new station could only be reached by an incline of 1 in 42 downwards. Rope haulage was introduced from the start, so this at least reduced sulphur levels, with much of the climb taking place in tunnel. By 1909 this practice was ended, partly because locomotives were obviously much more powerful than in the 1840s, but rope haulage required the loco firemen to walk along the frames when in motion, to ascertain that the rope collar had fallen away cleanly, and this was too dangerous a practice for even the Edwardians to stomach. However, the accumulation in the tunnel of steam and smoke from engines working hard – two per train – made Queen Street an unpleasant place to begin or end a train journey in the days of steam.

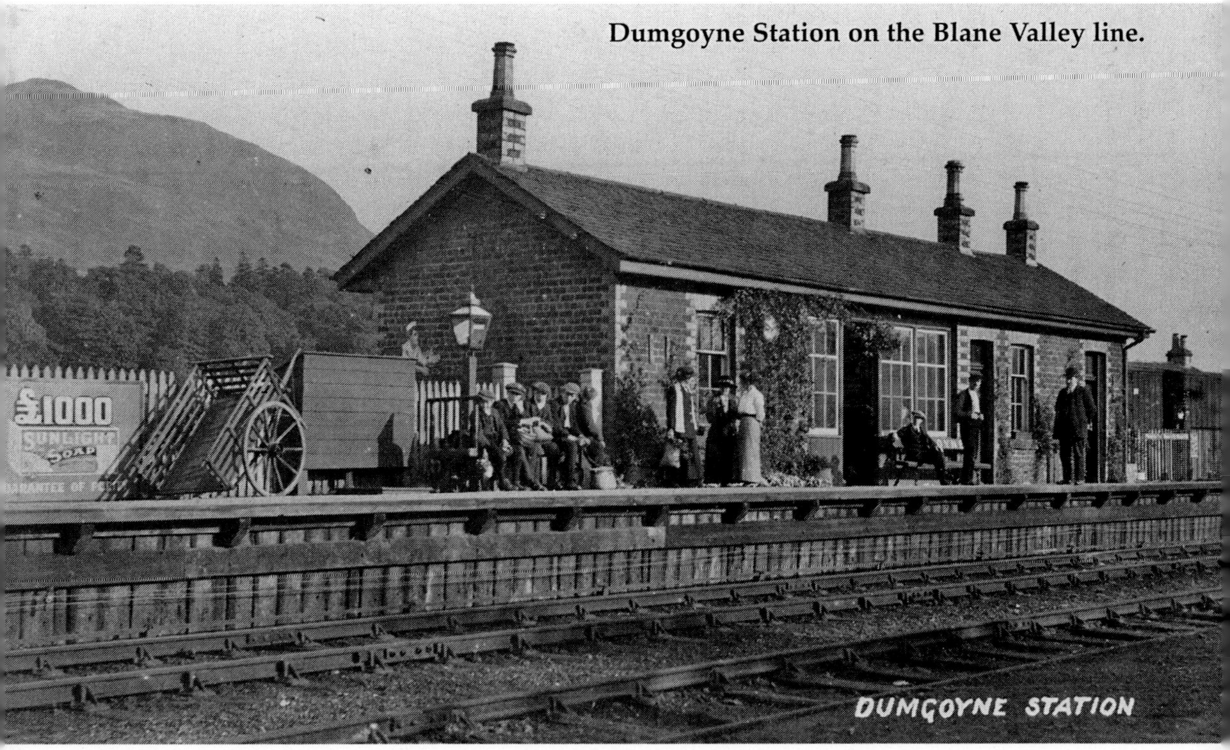

Dumgoyne Station on the Blane Valley line.

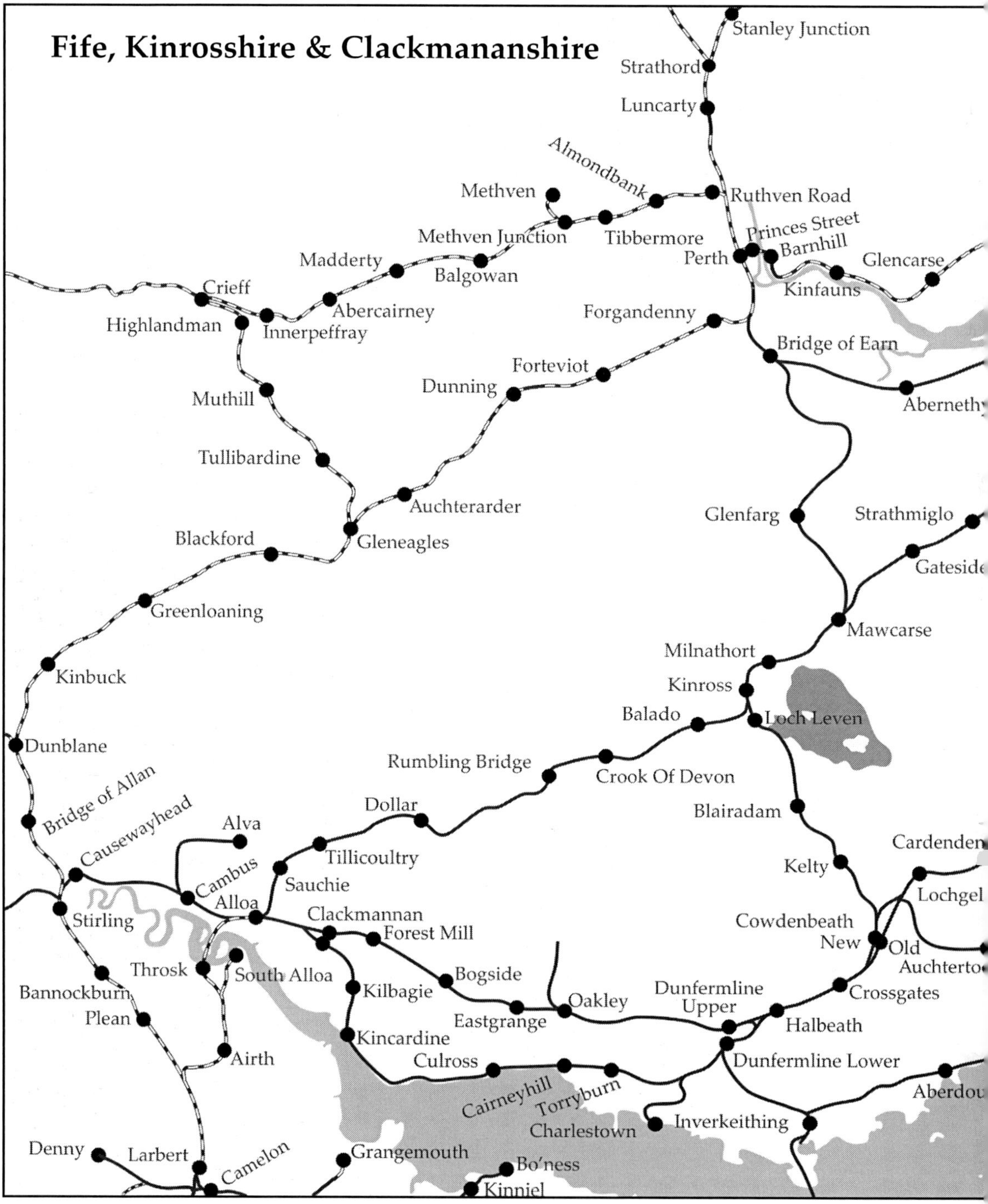
Fife, Kinrosshire & Clackmananshire
Stanley Junction
Strathord
Luncarty
Almondbank
Methven
Ruthven Road
Methven Junction
Tibbermore
Princes Street
Barnhill
Perth
Glencarse
Madderty
Balgowan
Kinfauns
Crieff
Abercairney
Forgandenny
Highlandman
Innerpeffray
Bridge of Earn
Forteviot
Dunning
Muthill
Abernethy
Tullibardine
Auchterarder
Glenfarg
Strathmiglo
Blackford
Gleneagles
Gateside
Greenloaning
Mawcarse
Milnathort
Kinbuck
Kinross
Balado
Loch Leven
Dunblane
Rumbling Bridge
Crook Of Devon
Bridge of Allan
Blairadam
Dollar
Causewayhead
Alva
Cardenden
Tillicoultry
Kelty
Cambus
Sauchie
Lochgel
Alloa
Stirling
Clackmannan
Cowdenbeath
Forest Mill
New
Old
Throsk
South Alloa
Bogside
Auchterto
Kilbagie
Dunfermline
Upper
Crossgates
Bannockburn
Oakley
Plean
Eastgrange
Halbeath
Kincardine
Dunfermline Lower
Airth
Culross
Cairneyhill
Torryburn
Aberdou
Charlestown
Inverkeithing
Denny
Larbert
Camelon
Grangemouth
Bo'ness
Kinniel

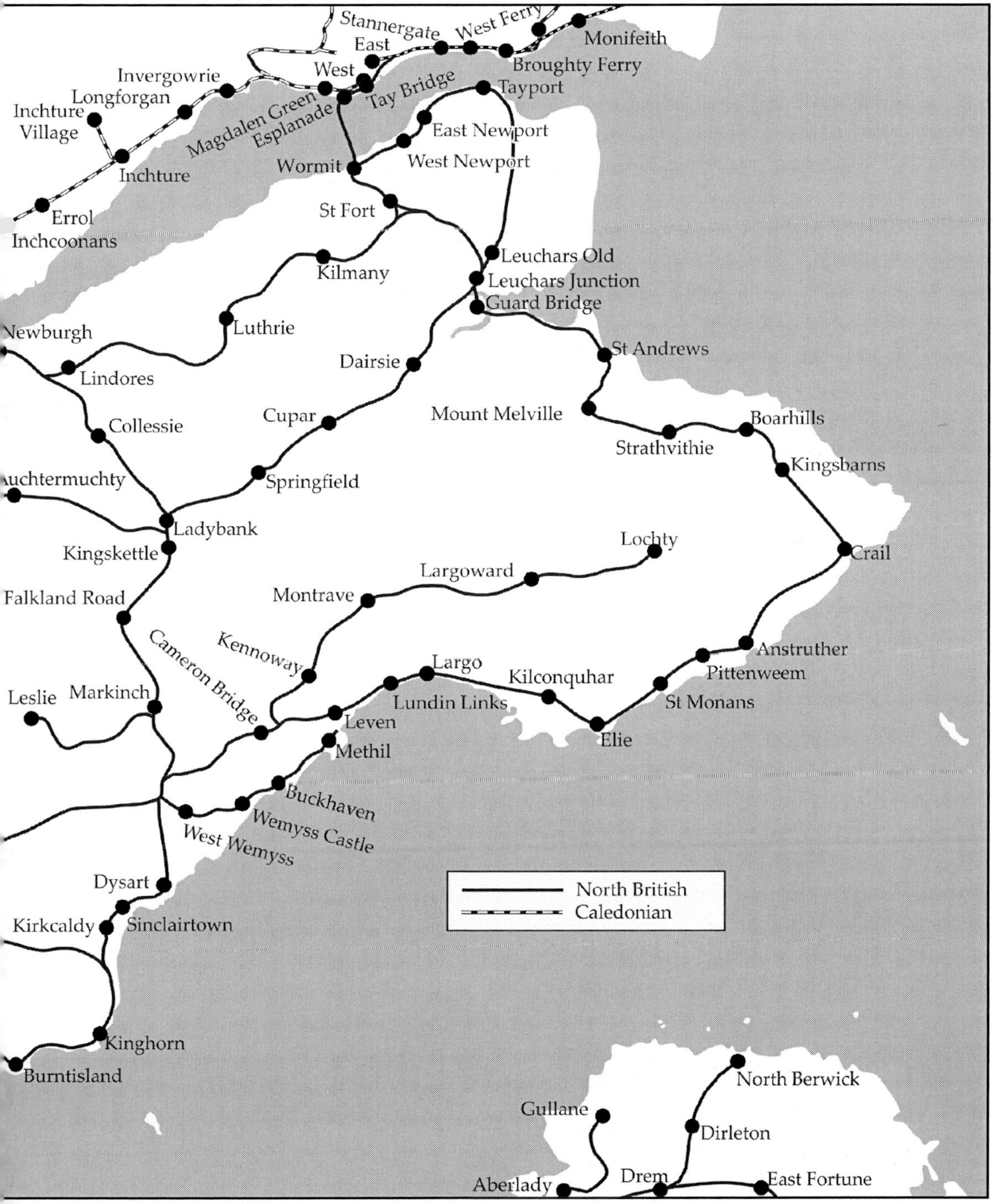

Stannergate
West Ferry
East
Monifeith
Broughty Ferry
Invergowrie
West
Tay Bridge
Tayport
Longforgan
Inchture Village
Magdalen Green
Esplanade
East Newport
West Newport
Wormit
Inchture
Errol
Inchcoonans
St Fort
Leuchars Old
Kilmany
Leuchars Junction
Guard Bridge
Newburgh
Luthrie
St Andrews
Dairsie
Lindores
Mount Melville
Cupar
Boarhills
Collessie
Strathvithie
Kingsbarns
uchtermuchty
Springfield
Ladybank
Kingskettle
Lochty
Crail
Largoward
Falkland Road
Montrave
Kennoway
Cameron Bridge
Anstruther
Pittenweem
Largo
Kilconquhar
Leslie
Markinch
Lundin Links
St Monans
Leven
Elie
Methil
Buckhaven
Wemyss Castle
West Wemyss
North British
Caledonian
Dysart
Kirkcaldy
Sinclairtown
Kinghorn
Burntisland
North Berwick
Gullane
Dirleton
Drem
East Fortune
Aberlady

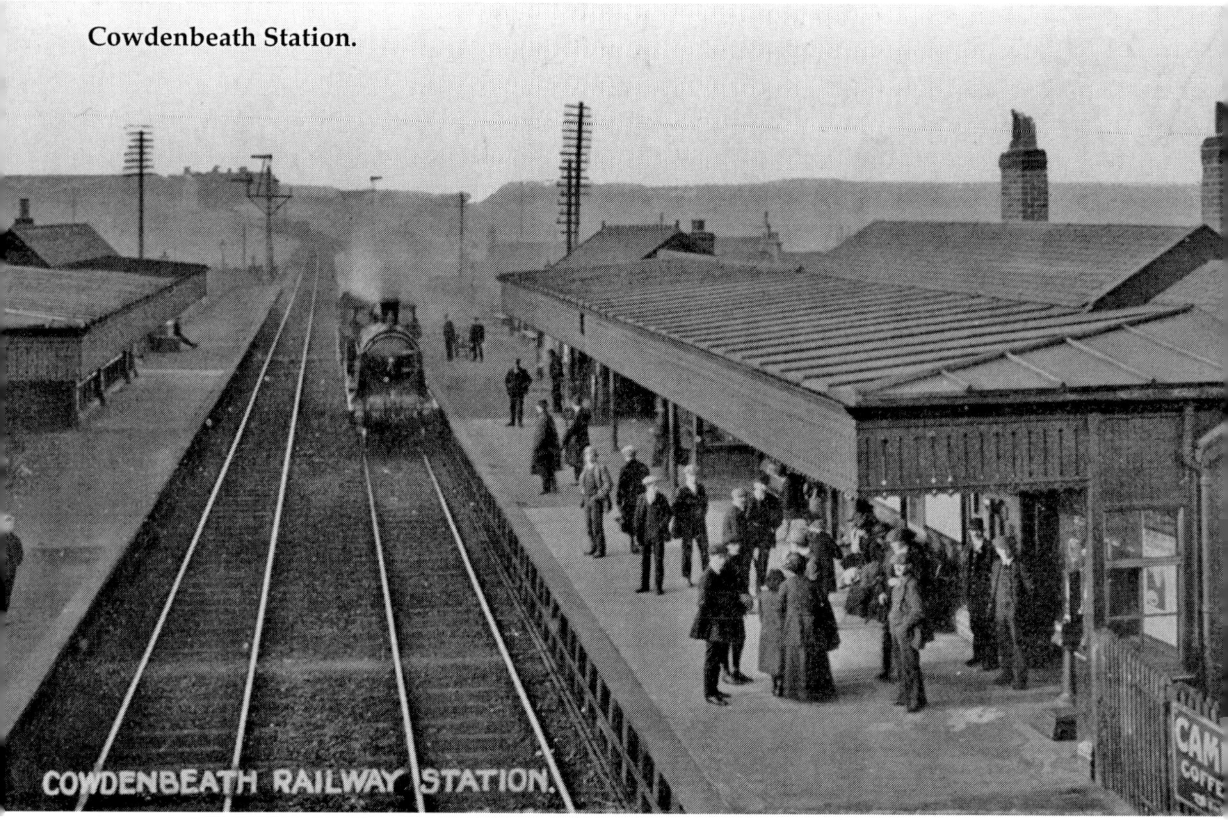

Cowdenbeath Station.

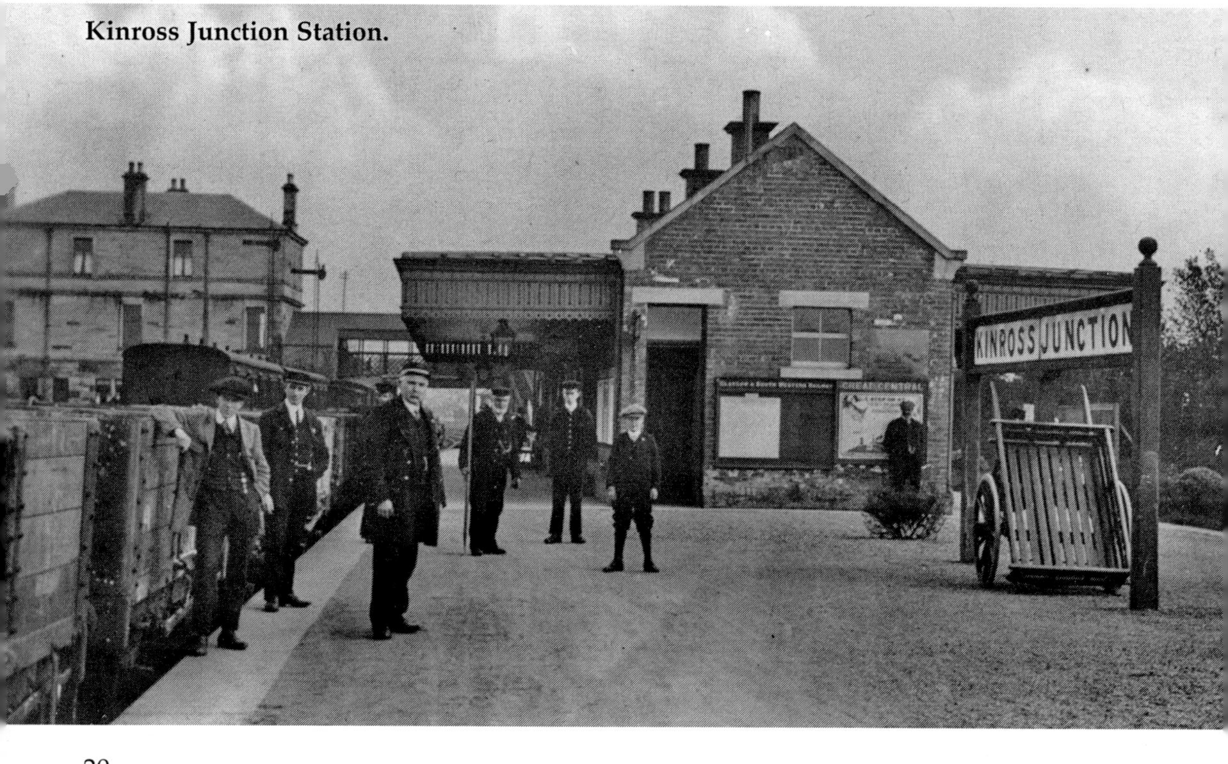

Kinross Junction Station.

North and West

By 1865, the North British Railway could almost have renamed itself the Edinburgh and South Eastern! While it did stretch one tentacle towards Glasgow, reached through Bathgate and Airdrie, the company's main line still ran no farther than from Edinburgh to Berwick. True, the Edinburgh-Carlisle 'Waverley Route', opened three years earlier, was longer, but it generated little traffic, and was described quite openly as a "drain on the rest of the system" in a company publication. West of Edinburgh, there was a line to Larbert, and in Fife, NBR rails stretched from Forth to Tay. In terms of a passenger network, it was less than impressive, but the company could content itself that, if passengers' fares did not meet costs, Scotland's mineral traffic certainly would.

In those days, there was a major export market for Scottish coal, and the NBR was able to move black diamonds from the West Lothian and Lanarkshire fields, while enjoying a near-monopoly of those in Fife and Midlothian. Bo'ness, Methil, and Leith were the principal points of export, all of them invested in by the NBR, and the company could expedite domestic supplies into the two biggest cities as well as Perth. Any English demand could be supplied at three places where NBR metals crossed the Border (Berwick, the North Tyne, Carlisle), but 1865 was to produce an event which was to change the company, making it one of the biggest players in the British transport market.

If there was one company which was expected to take over the Edinburgh & Glasgow Railway, it was the Caledonian. The latter's trains to and from the south required to traverse former Monkland Railway metals in travelling between the South and Greenhill, near Falkirk. Not surprisingly, the 'Caley' had focused on acquiring the E & G, and this amalgamation (effectively a takeover by the 'Caley') came so close to fruition that the two companies' trade results were bracketed together by the investors' press for many years. All to no avail – the Monkland was taken over by the E & G, along with the Union Canal, the day before it was absorbed by the North British, in 1865.

The Almond Valley Viaduct on the Edinburgh and Glasgow Railway.

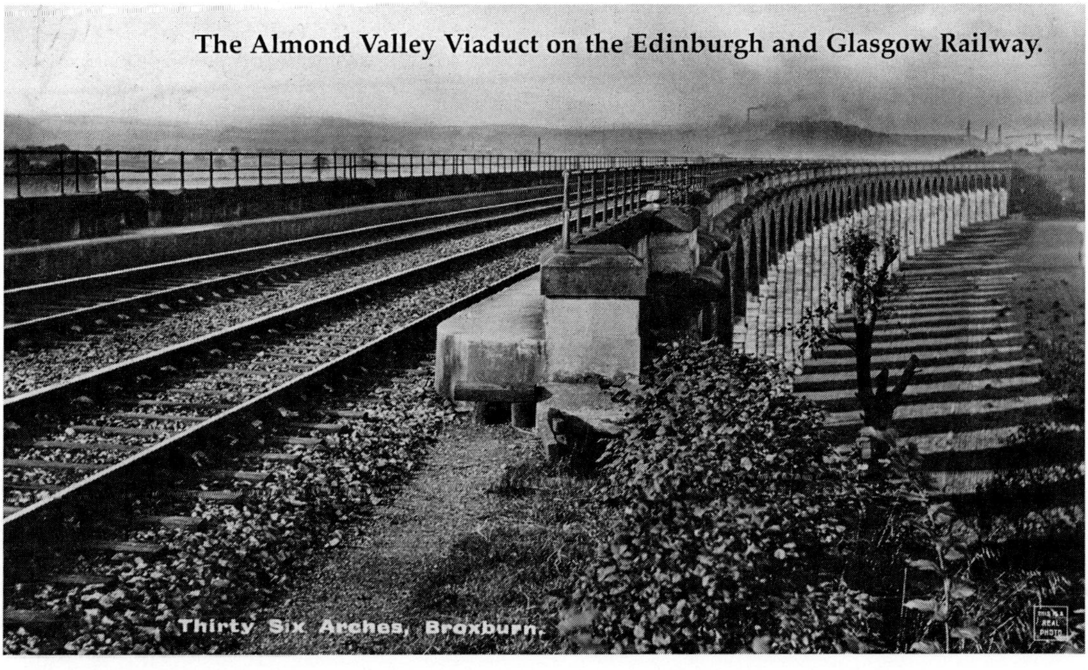

The Edinburgh and Glasgow Railway was the 'Liverpool and Manchester' of Scotland. It was the first trunk line built north of the Border, and connected the two major cities from 1842, before either the NBR or Caledonian ran their first trains. Running across a narrow isthmus between two important cities, it should have been a high-earning company. It fact, it was not. Like many railway concerns at the time, the E & G was badly run. Its management was one of the poorest in the country – which was saying something – and its board had made the nonsensical decision to tackle competition from the waterway system by lowering fares, instead of concentrating on their strength, namely speed, which of course the two canals (the Forth & Clyde connecting with the Union) could not possibly match.

The Caledonian failed to accomplish the merger in 1850 when, in financial difficulties, it agreed that the parity of the amalgamation terms should be based on the frequency of train services between Edinburgh and Glasgow. To achieve this, the 'Caley' effectively became the E & G's rival, attempting to exceed the older company's service frequency and (already unremuneratively low fare structure) when ill-equipped to do so.

An opportunity was left for the NBR to exploit, but the latter company was unable to take advantage until 1865. The fact that NBR chairman John Learmonth had been ejected from the E & G boardroom in 1846 by an uprising of Sabbatarian shareholders, doubtless gave that gentleman great satisfaction in renewing his contact with the older company. The NBR also felt the effects of the pressure group determined to stop Sunday travel. Indeed,

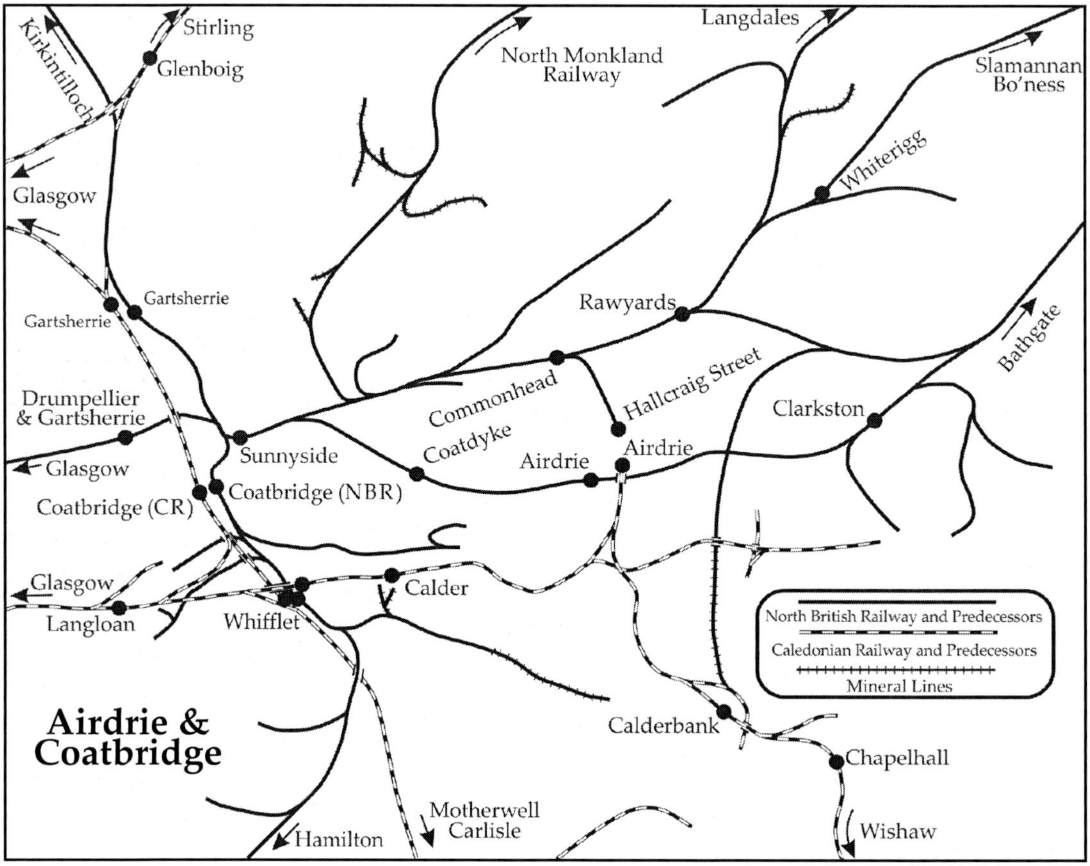

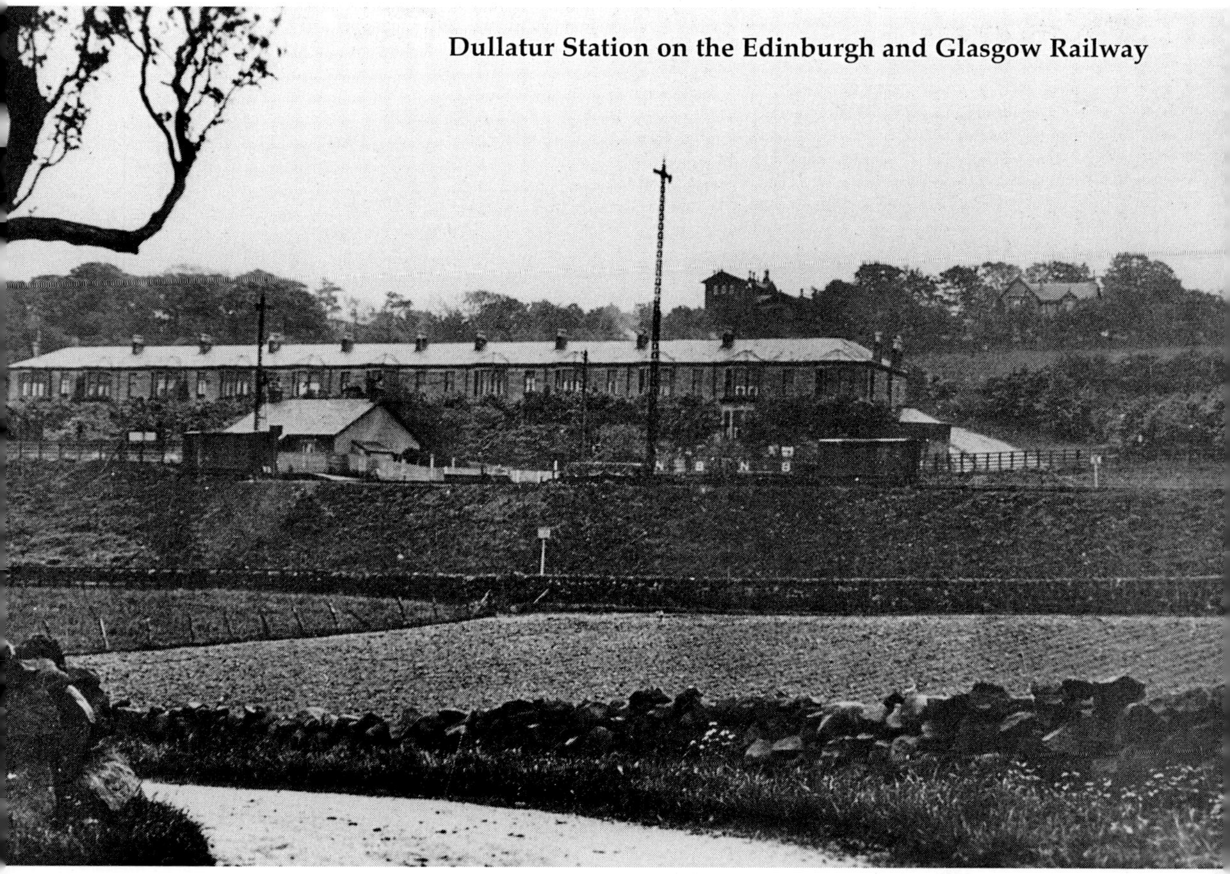

Dullatur Station on the Edinburgh and Glasgow Railway

only the death of William IV in 1837 had prevented Sabbatarian legislation being enacted which would have outlawed any kind of Sunday activity, apart from actions designed to save life.

The 1865 NBR/E & G merger, takeover, call it what you will, was a triumph for the North British. At a stroke it acquired a straight, almost entirely level main line between Edinburgh and Glasgow. It now had a terminus within a porter's shout of the city's George Square. It acquired Cowlairs Works, in addition to its existing plants at St. Margaret's and Burntisland, both of which now became secondary to the Glasgow site.

The NBR could now offer its English partners on the East Coast main line an additional destination for their trains – one bigger than any English provincial city apart from Birmingham, and Britain's first sleeping-car service would start from Glasgow's Queen Street within a few years. A route to the north-west now beckoned, serving not just north Clydeside, but the entire West Highlands. In time the NBR pushed northwards not just to Fort William, but to Mallaig and Fort Augustus, within 35 miles of Inverness. The merger even brought the NBR its own canal, the Union, connecting Edinburgh with the Forth and Clyde Canal at Falkirk. Last, but by no means least, the strip of Monkland line required by the Caledonian for its Carlisle-Aberdeen services was now in NBR hands, ensuring that the latter company had to negotiate running-powers with the NBR, who in turn could expect the 'Caley' to be much more amenable in permitting NBR trains into Aberdeen! The North British Railway had really arrived!

Central Scotland

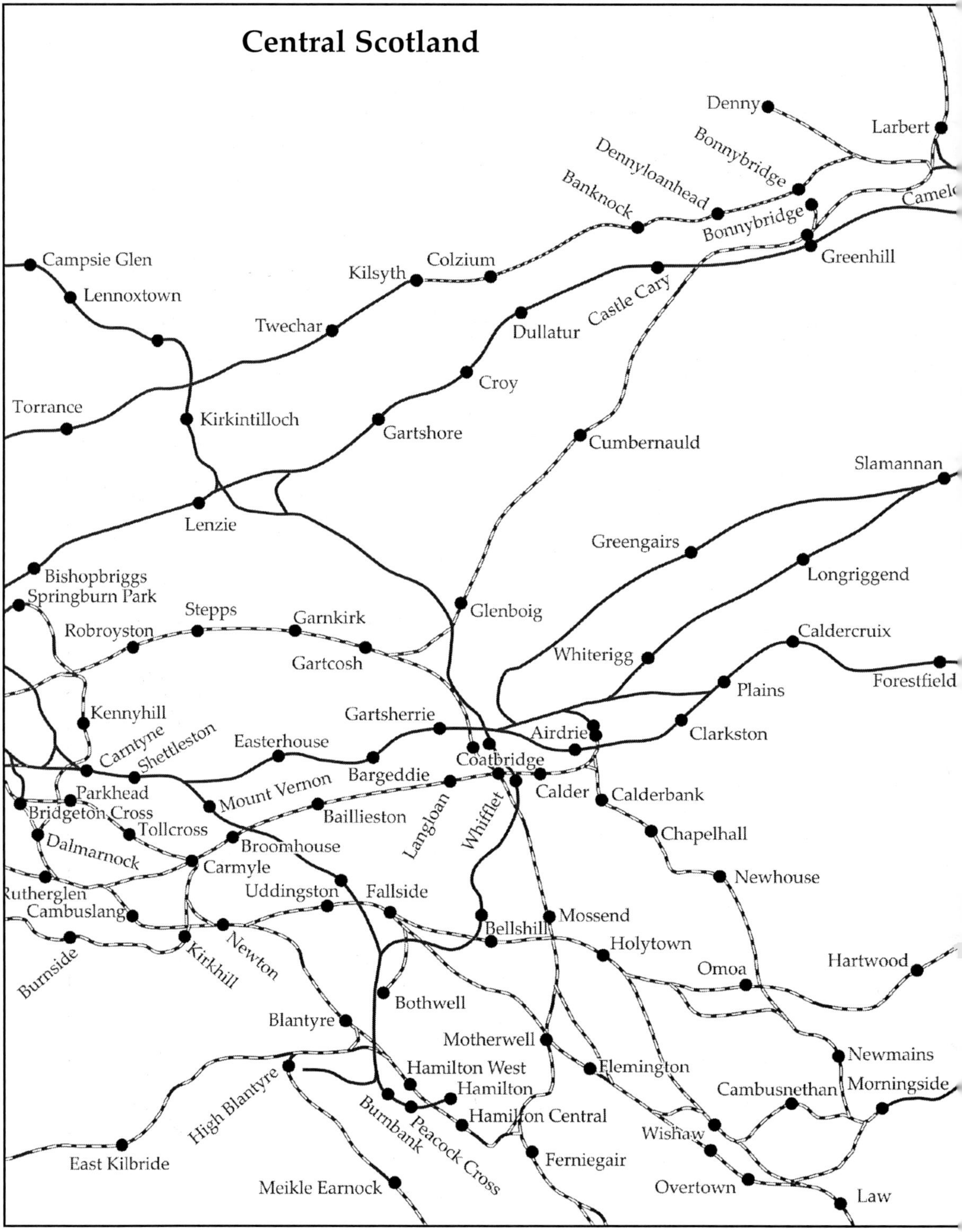

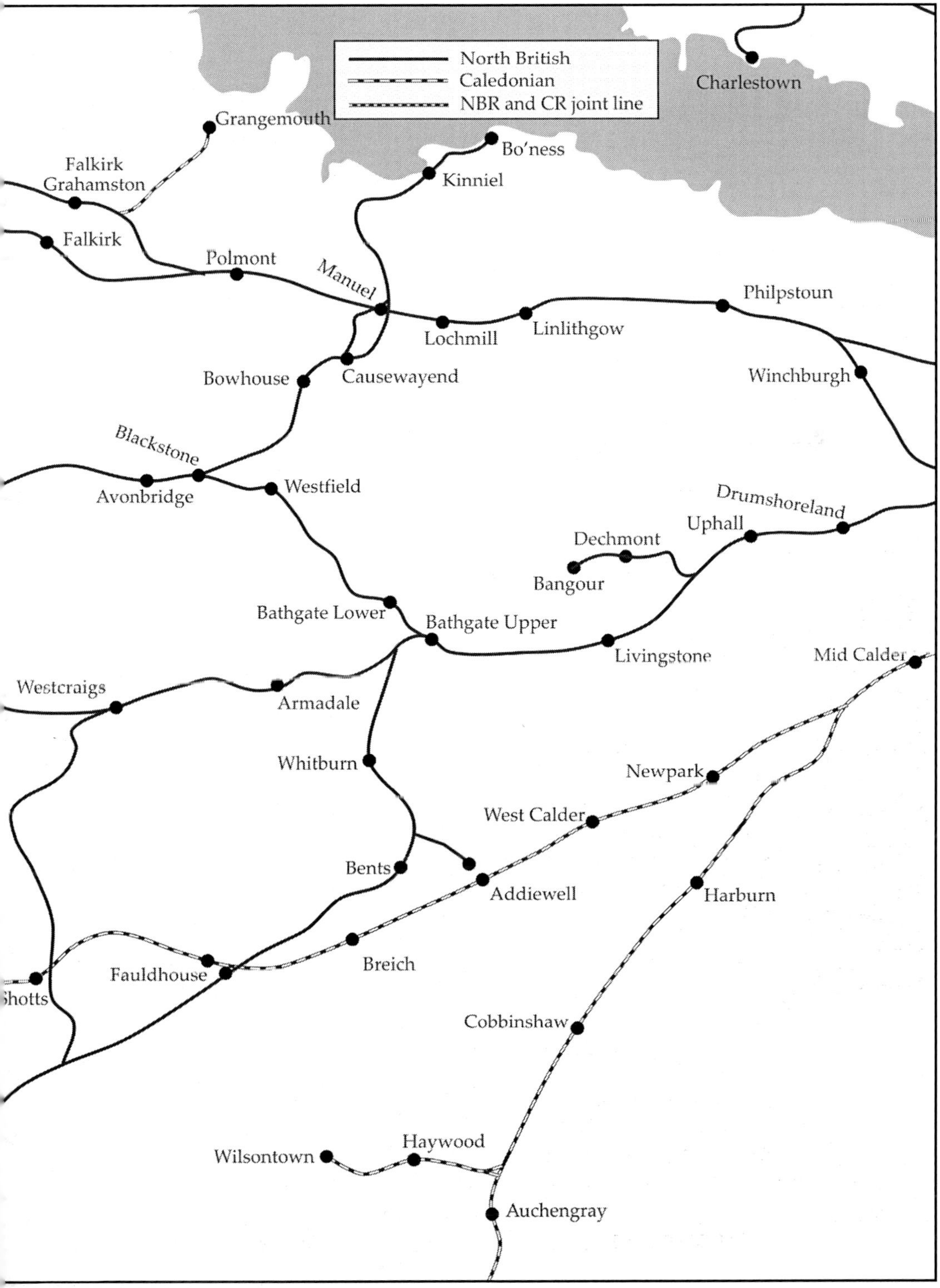
North British
Caledonian
NBR and CR joint line
Charlestown
Grangemouth
Bo'ness
Kinniel
Falkirk
Grahamston
Falkirk
Polmont
Manuel
Philpstoun
Lochmill
Linlithgow
Bowhouse
Causewayend
Winchburgh
Blackstone
Avonbridge
Westfield
Drumshoreland
Uphall
Dechmont
Bangour
Bathgate Lower
Bathgate Upper
Livingstone
Mid Calder
Westcraigs
Armadale
Whitburn
Newpark
West Calder
Bents
Addiewell
Harburn
Breich
Fauldhouse
hotts
Cobbinshaw
Haywood
Wilsontown
Auchengray

Completing the Waverley Route

The Waverley Route between Edinburgh and Carlisle closed in 1969, yet it still exercises a tug on the sleeve of any imaginative railway enthusiast. Unlike the closure of some duplicatory main lines in England – the spine of the Great Central, or the former LSWR in north Devon and Cornwall – this closure completely deprived a number of towns of any railway service. It was just as well that Hawick citizens reputedly liked to stay at home anyway, for they now no station nearer than Berwick-on-Tweed 35 miles away. On one occasion in the 1970s a strike by bus crews meant that the best part of 100,000 people in the Central Borders had no public transport service at all.

To the railway enthusiast, the Waverley Route had an almost romantic air. Here could be seen graceful Pacifics or powerful Diesels pounding or grinding uphill at speeds of around 30 mph, crossing a number of lengthy viaducts across empty valleys, amid smooth hillsides barren of a single tree. Although only 98 miles in length – slightly shorter than the Caledonian line – not many trains could compete with the 'Caley' for speed by this route. For the 'Caley's Beattock bank, the Waverley Route had two of similar length and steepness, Falahill and Whitrope. The *Elizabethan* express headed by an A4 Pacific in good nick was recorded taking 162 minutes when diverted on to this line; the author once timed a Class 46 Diesel in 166 minutes, admittedly with stops.

It was as if the directors of the North British Railway *enjoyed* building railways where none existed before, and where nobody else would ever envisage the need for one!

The Waverley Route was built in two phases. The infant NBR was determined to run before it could walk in the mid-1840s, deciding to build a branch to Hawick while still constructing its principal line connecting Edinburgh with Berwick. Its takeover of the mineral lines of the Edinburgh and Dalkeith gave it a launch-pad into the Borders, immediately allowing the new company as far as Newtongrange nine miles south of

Tynehead Station on the Waverley Route

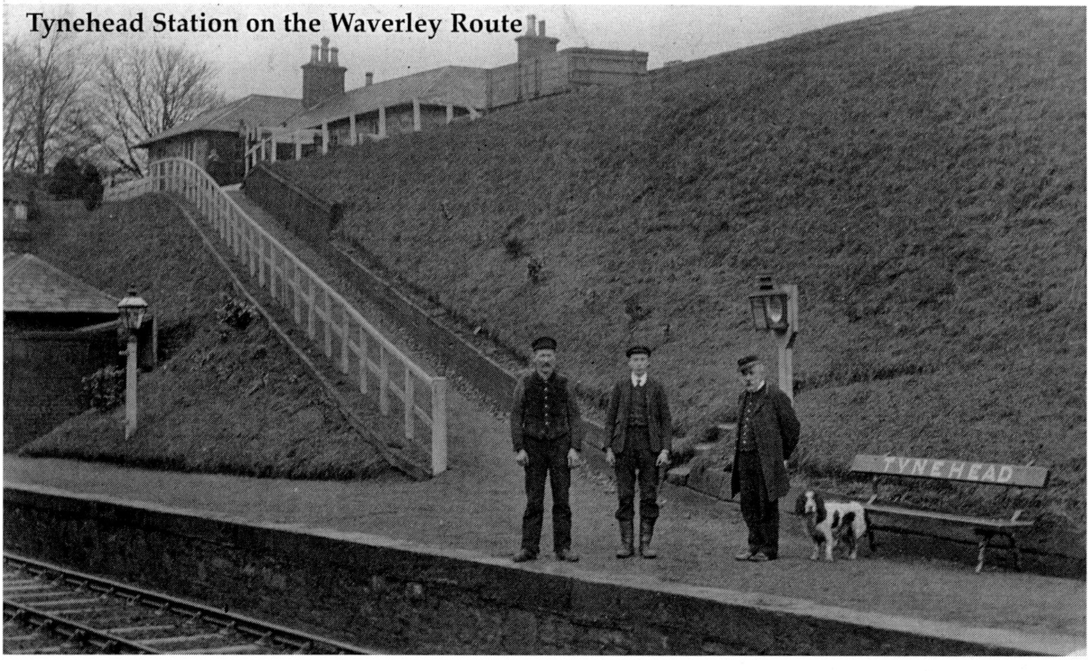

Hawthornden Station on the Peebles Railway.

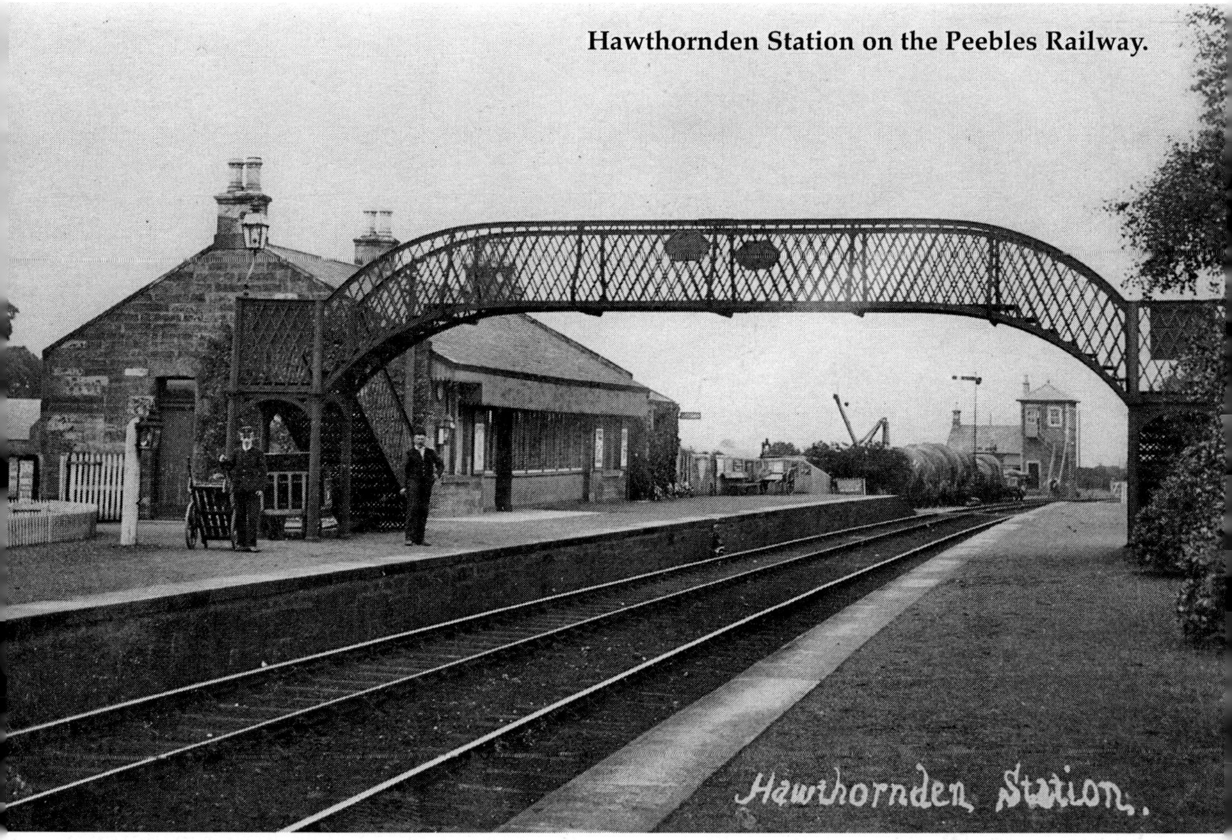

Edinburgh, and this may have encouraged the directors to be over-optimistic of the physical challenges ahead. They soon learned the reality of messing with the Border hills. Borthwick Bank on the climb to the Falahill pass proved to be a major earthwork – it still is, forming a curtain wall across the valley which once connected Crichton and Borthwick Castles. The Gala Water had to be bridged seven times, and the Tweed once, and that was only in the first 35 miles! Not surprisingly, getting rails into Hawick nearly bankrupted the NBR and the traffic generated proved simply not worth the effort. To be viable, the line had to reach Carlisle, and in 1849, with the North British exhausted, the Border must have seemed a very long way away.

Before proceeding with the chronology of the story, perhaps a brief pen picture of this lost main line is appropriate.

The Waverley Route left the East Coast main line at Portobello East Junction, $3^1/_2$ miles from Waverley Station. The junction still exists today, used by the new Border Line services, but no longer to London (St. Pancras). Few passers-by would imagine that this was where the concept of remote railway signalling began.

In 1847, Robert Skelden, appointed by the NBR to operate two signals by hand, decided to save his energy by using discarded track chairs to rig up a mechanical method of operating signals from a distance, and centralising the necessary levers. His ingenuity earned him a medal 'worth five sovereigns' from the Royal Scottish Society of Arts on November 2nd 1849 – yet the North British company's first reaction was to consider sacking him for laziness! Whether

Skelden was copying a pioneering interlocking scheme at Bricklayer's Arms in London is not known; the Society was obviously impressed, whether he was a true pioneer or not. Portobello East later featured as the 'winning post' in a railway race.

From Portobello, the Waverley Route climbed southwards through Niddrie North and South Junctions and past Millerhill Station. This was chosen as a site for a marshalling yard in the 1950s, providing Scotland with one of its most unnecessary transport facilities, and wasting hundreds of acres of agricultural land. The line crossed the North and South Esk rivers west of Dalkeith, with a branch running into a very central terminus in the town (which failed to stop it closing to passengers as early as 1942). Just south of here, a branch trailed in from the East Lothian coalfield, and a passenger branch went off to the west at Hardengreen. At one time this offered services to Penicuik and Glencorse, that area of Midlothian, along with Roslin, enjoying a complicated network of branch lines up until closure to passengers in 1951. The fact that Penicuik's population had grown fourfold by then, passed un-noticed by railway administrators. Even more importantly, a branch left Hardengreen for Peebles. Financed privately to begin with, it was eventually taken over by the NBR who extended it to Galashiels via Innerleithen, thus providing a loop off the Waverley Route. A most scenic line it was too, so naturally British Railways closed it as soon as they decently could, in 1962, the biggest railway to be demolished in Scotland up to that time.

Meanwhile, the Waverley line mounted the Moorfoot Hills, crossing the watershed at Falahill. The author recalls travelling in a St. Pancras-bound express one morning in the 1950s, finding it unbelievable that our V2 locomotive was making such heavy weather of the climb. To its credit, it picked up speed so quickly after the summit, that the scenery of the Gala Water, the villages of Heriot, Fountainhall (the latter with what remained of its junction for Lauder), and Stow, went past in a blur.

Galashiels (33 miles from Edinburgh) would describe itself as the most important town in the Borders, a claim that is renewed, somewhat differently, when you later arrive in Hawick!

Work on the Esk Viaduct in 1912.

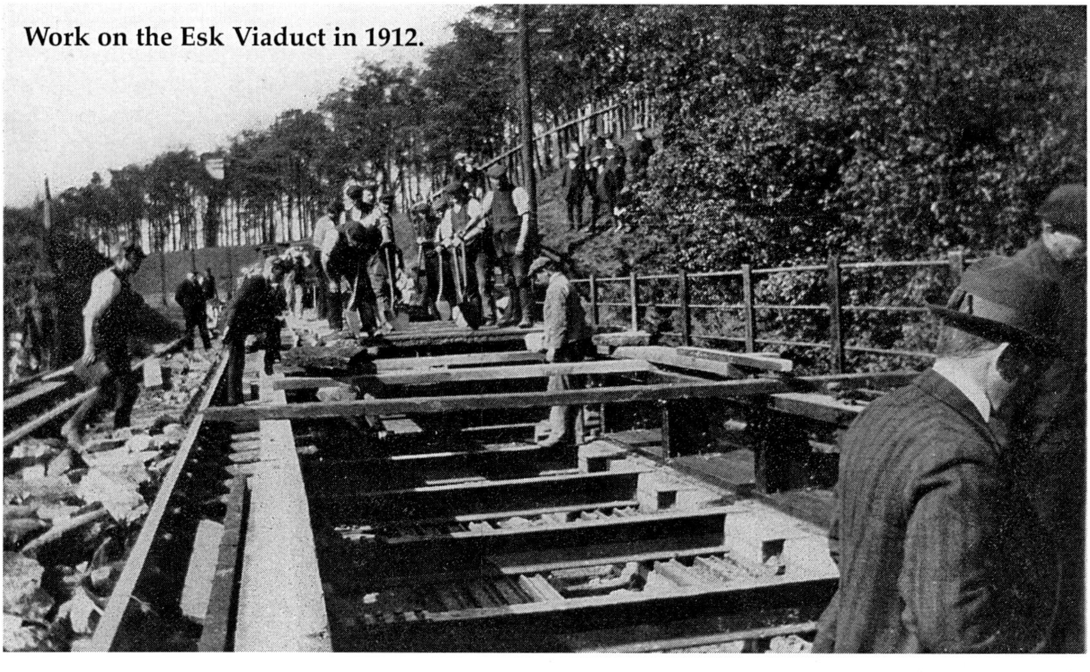

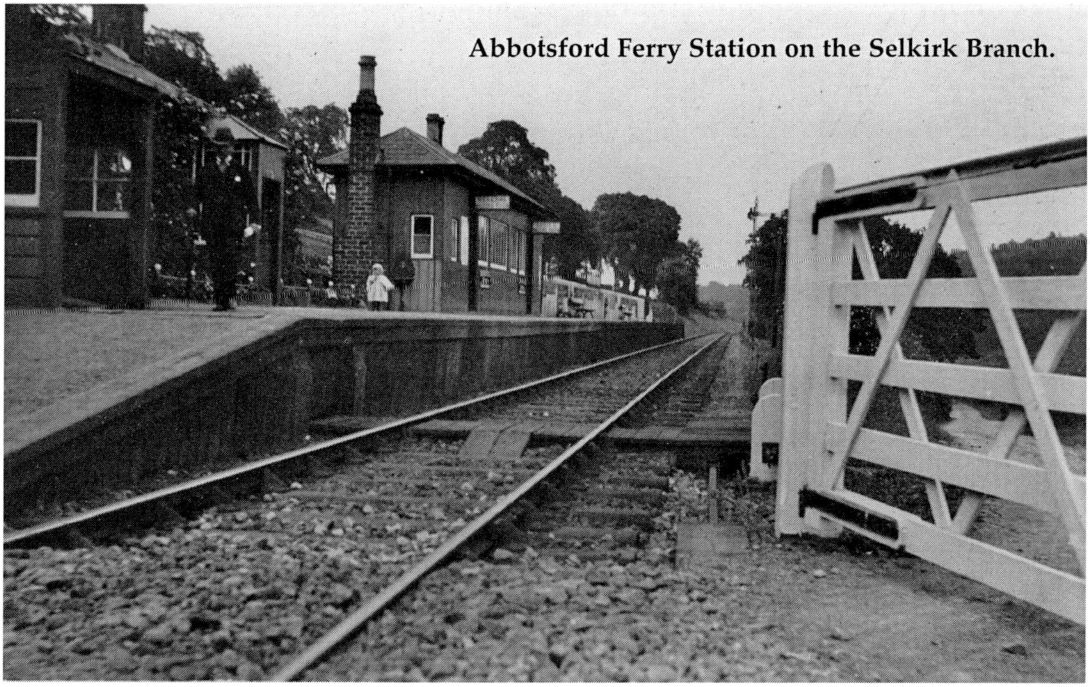

Gala was an important textile centre, and its station acted as a junction point for two branch services – back to Edinburgh via Innerleithen and Peebles (this being the loop which left the Waverley line at Hardengreen), and to Selkirk. The former closed to passengers in 1962, the latter some 11 years earlier. Not long after leaving Galashiels, the main line crossed the Tweed by an impressive single-arch bridge which cost the NBR no less than £5,000 to construct at a time of a serious trade recession.

The line southwards from here to Hawick was unique on the Waverley Route in not involving any heavy climbing for trains in either direction. Not that this made for easier railroading – the problem about the line was that it was not just steeply graded, with two near-1,000 foot summits, but that it included tortuous curvature. Melrose Station need not be written about in the past tense as its buildings are still largely intact on one side of what is effectively the Melrose by-pass at this point.

Passengers travelling south on the line would now be anticipating a glimpse of the elegant Leaderfoot Viaduct bringing the Duns and Reston line trailing in at Ravenswood Junction, just north of St. Boswells. The 19-arch viaduct is preserved nowadays, and it's perhaps a miracle that it has lasted so long, as the Board of Trade inspection in 1864 was unbelievably casual. Within six months, the structure was having to receive emergency bracing in iron and concrete, emergency works which are still perfectly visible. Fortunately, loadings on the viaduct were never heavy, and now closed off, it remains as a fine Borders landmark, a monument to Victorian optimism, if not to Victorian engineering.

St. Boswells was the next stop, almost halfway down the line, and with branch lines going off to north-east and south-east. They were in fact both through routes, the Duns line joining the East Coast main line at Reston Junction, where, even until the time of closure to passengers in 1951, trains had to make a reversal before they could occupy Reston's bay

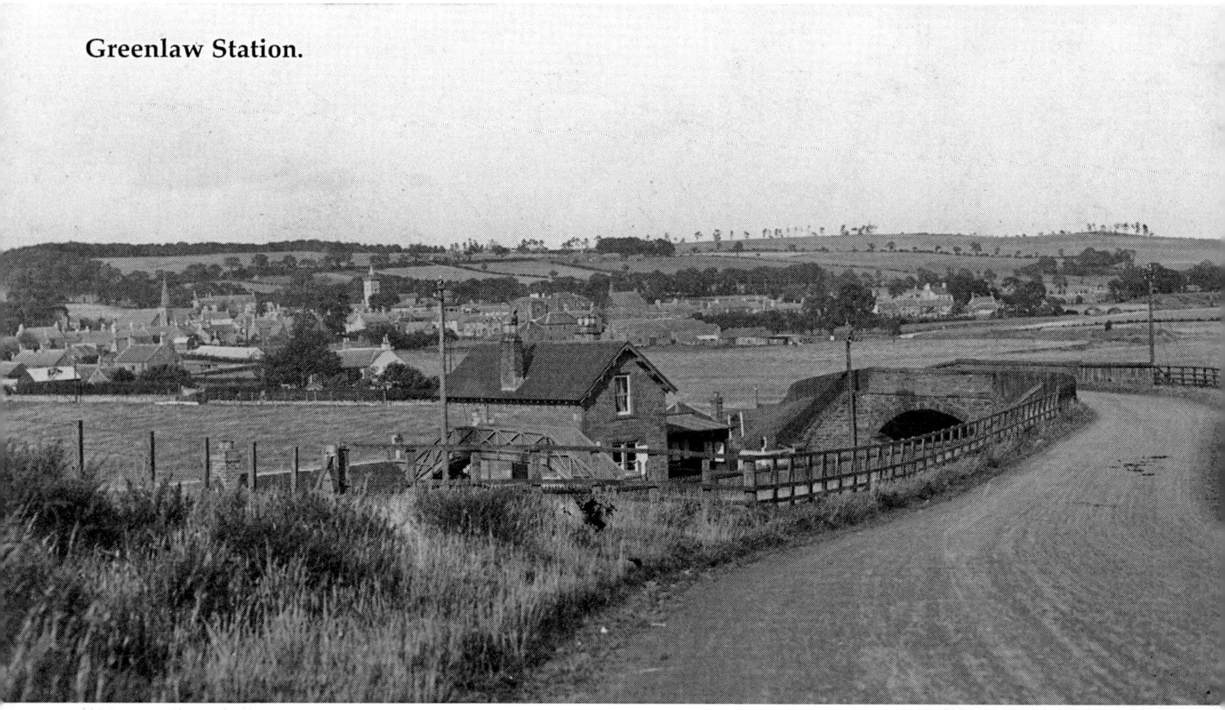

Greenlaw Station.

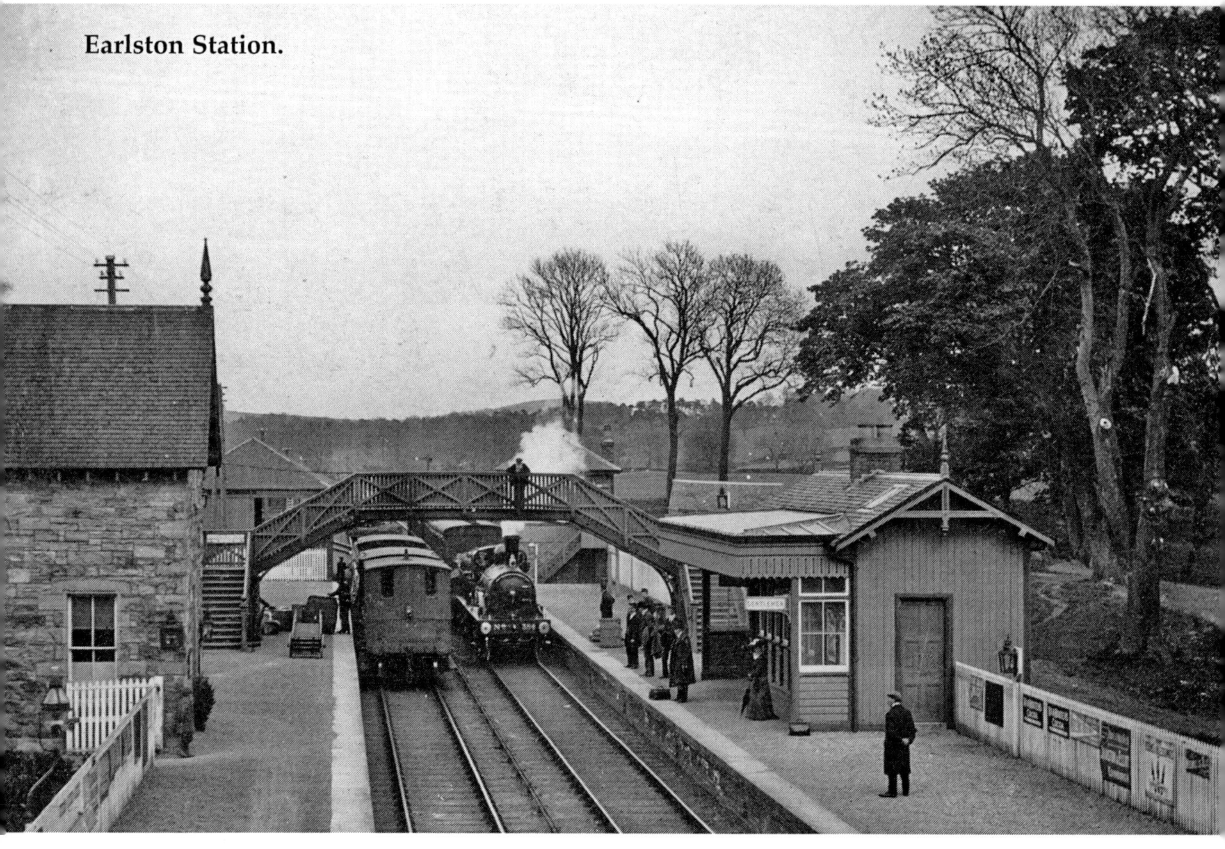

Earlston Station.

platform. Not too surprisingly, when the last Duns-Reston service steamed out, not a single resident turned up to wave it goodbye.

Also starting from here were trains for Kelso, which (usually after a long wait at that town) eventually found their way to Tweedmouth. Because of its junctions' configurations, this was a useful deviation route, particularly in 1948, when rain washed out so many East Coast bridges. In that bedraggled summer and autumn, Haymarket enginemen operating the non-stop 'Flying Scotsman', with their A4 Pacifics, succeeded in taking the crack express along this extra mileage without once having to stop for water – a marvellous feat of railroading undertaken without official sanction. Indeed, we do not know how many times this record (408.6 miles non-stop) was achieved; the previous figure of 17 journeys having to be upgraded in the light of new research. Readers are recommended to consult detailed articles on these two lines published in 2000 and 2002 respectively – see 'Works Consulted'.

A branch to Jedburgh left the St. Boswells-Kelso line at Roxburgh Junction, its closure in 1948 inevitable because of the effects on the rainfall on the line's bridges. The authorities were obviously happy to see it go, with their unadventurous timetabling and the operation of a terminus too far from the heart of the community it purported to serve.

Belses and Hassendean were the two stations between St. Boswells and Hawick, passengers enjoying views of the Eildon Hills to the west and later the Minto Hills to the east. There was a summit at Standhill – minor by Waverley Route standards – and trains were soon rolling past Burnfoot, into Hawick. When they first did this in 1849, the station building was decked with evergreens and flags. This was later to become the goods shed and was configured to allow a line to continue along the west bank of the Teviot and then southwards. Unfortunately for the North British Railway, financially exhausted by his expenditure over the previous four years, this was not to be.

The Act of Parliament in 1845 which gave official status to the Caledonian Railway allowed it, belatedly, to begin constructing its main line northwards from Carlisle. It also allowed it to plan a plethora of branch lines, spurs, and triangular junctions in the area between Gretna Green and Longtown. While the company's promoters were doubtless genuinely keen to build two completely separate railways from Carlisle and Gretna to Canonbie, a village with a single coal-mine, the legislation allowing them to do so also enabled them to occupy the ground where the rival GSWR company (although not yet so-named) wanted to bring its line from Dumfries into England and turn south-east to Carlisle.

The Act also neatly pre-empted any North British advance down from Hawick, through Langholm and Canonbie, and on to Carlisle. During the years the NB was stalled at Hawick, this was to prove an insurmountable problem.

The attempts by the NB to overcome the dog-in-the-manger attitude of the Caledonian company – which had no intention of building northwards to Hawick – are dealt with by this author in the book *Rails Across the Border*. Suffice to say that the NBR had to choose another route to Carlisle, attempting to put a positive spin on the problem by deciding that a route via the Slitrig and Liddel rivers would open a possible second approach into England. This could be achieved if the extended Waverley Route split high in the Cheviots, with one leg heading down towards Longtown and Carlisle, and the other to the North Tyne Valley and Hexham.

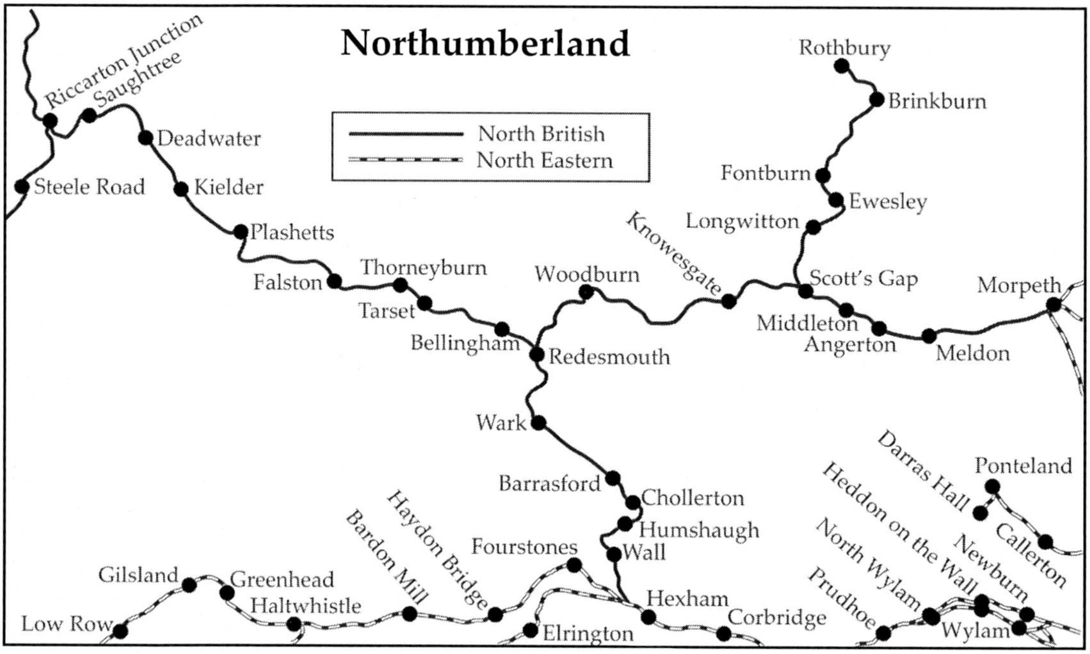

That was the *only* possible spin that this choice of route could suggest. To reach these twin destinations in England, the NBR had to realign its branch into Hawick across the Teviot, and then send it climbing round the east of the town and up into the Slitrig Valley. Impressive viaducts were required in the middle of Hawick, and at Lynnwood and Shankend, before further climbing was avoided by boring a 1,200 yard tunnel at Whitrope, before the summit of that name was reached. Shortly after, the North Tyne line (later known as the 'Border Counties Railway') went off at Riccarton, a spot so heavily-populated that no road had ever been required to reach it! Indeed, no public road ever did, the forestry authorities eventually sending a track into this remote part of Roxburghshire. The railway village which sprang up at Riccarton was supplied entirely by rail, with a co-operative shop in the station building and church services being held at one time in the engine shed.

Needless to say, both Riccarton and the Border Counties line leaving from there, became operational curiosities. The latter only occasionally carried any Edinburgh-Newcastle traffic, and such wayside stations of Deadwater, Kielder, and Plashetts generated virtually no revenue, either passenger or freight. A major part of the line now lies deep under the Bakethin and Kielder Reservoirs.

The Waverley Route is equally lost to modern mapmakers. From Riccarton, the line occupied an extensive – and expensive – earthwork to Newcastleton, a ducal village with a busy weaving industry. The villagers soon found themselves able to travel direct to London or Edinburgh without changing trains, while, over in the valley to the west, the larger community of Langholm had to make do with a branch line, from Riddings on the Waverley Route. Indeed, there is evidence that the NBR delayed building the branch, as if to punish the villagers for having supported the Caledonian's claim to build through the Mosspaul Pass!

Carlisle was reached through Longtown, with the NB joining its new constitutent, the Port Carlisle Branch, and then taking running powers over $1^{1}/_{4}$ miles of the Caledonian. The 'old enemy' charged for the powers on the basis of a four-mile occupancy, although the *Railway*

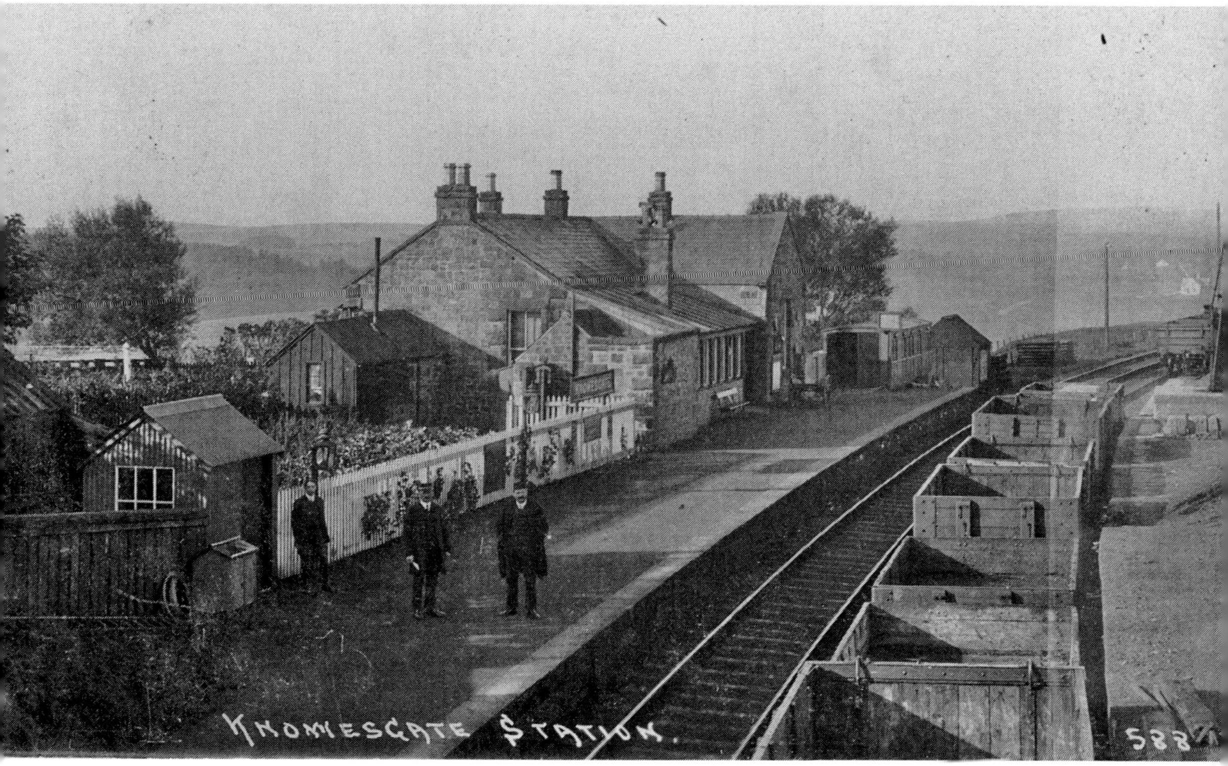
KNOWESGATE STATION.
588

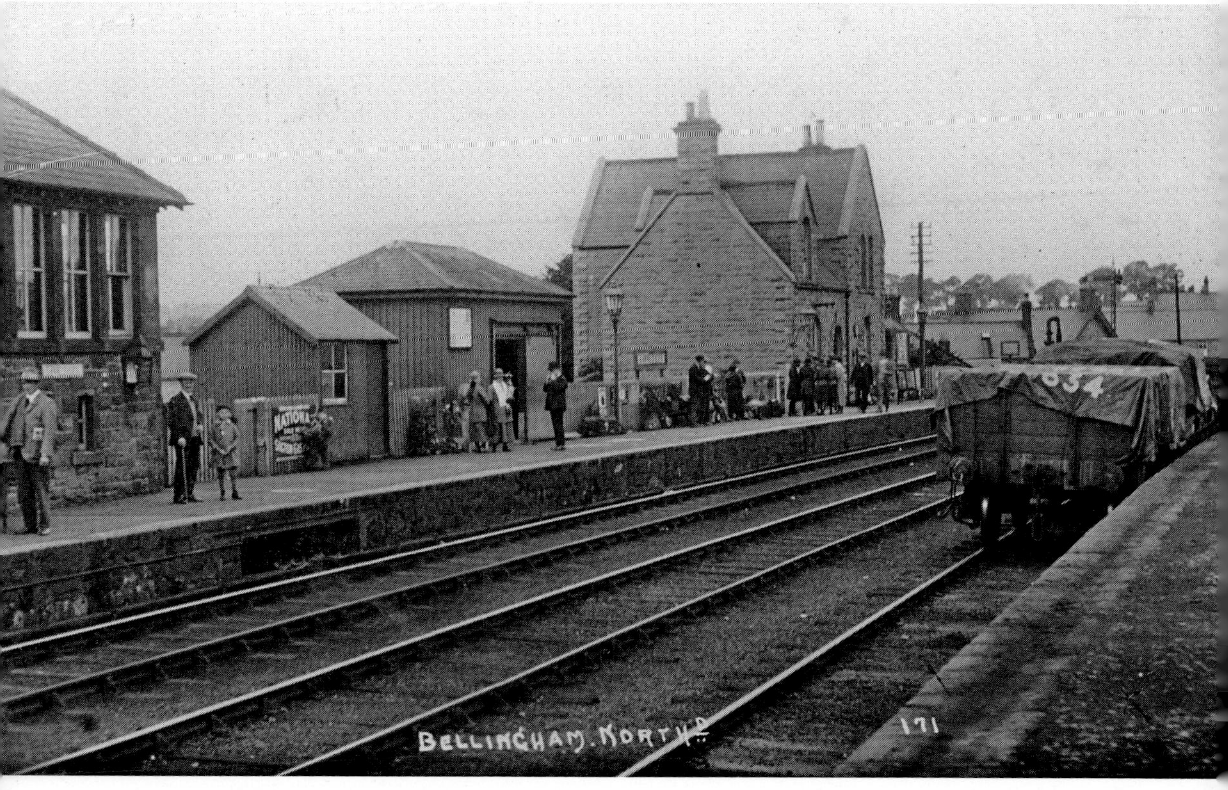
BELLINGHAM. NORTH'D
171
634

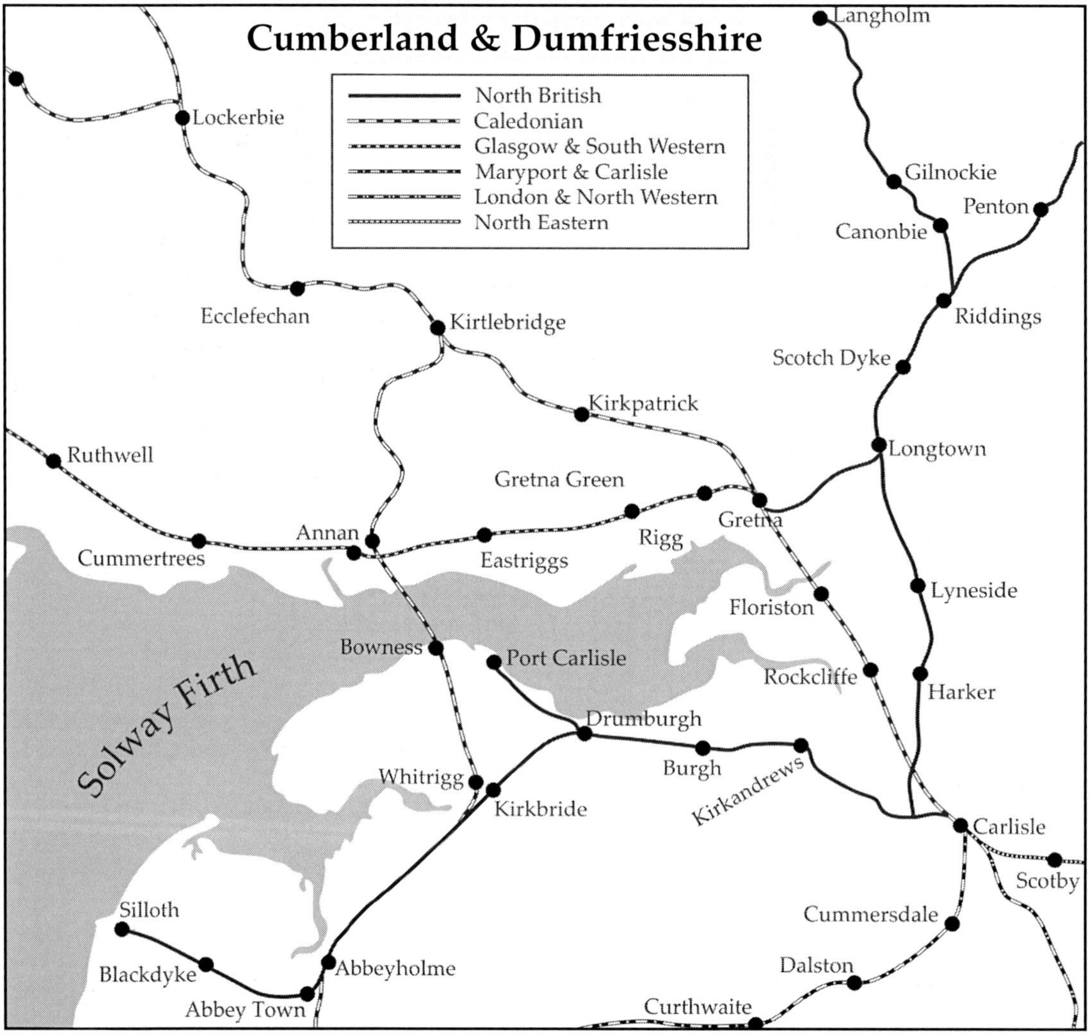

Times thought this a bargain, given the alternative costs of building a new approach into the crowded Border City.

So, North British trains were able to enter Carlisle Citadel for the first time in 1862. Unfortunately, there was no traffic from the south for them to collect – the London & North Western was allied to the Caledonian, and the Midland would not come into Carlisle for another 14 years.

In 1873, while the Midland was still trying to conquer the Pennine Fells in building its line from Settle to Carlisle, an independent committee of Scottish stockholders was looking at the possibility of a merger of the Caledonian and the North British. In giving evidence, the NB spokesman was quoted by the *Railway Times* as saying that his company would 'consider' a merger if the Caledonian would share equally the revenue of all Anglo-Scottish freight traffic through Carlisle, since the NB had gone to all the expense of providing an alternative route to the north. At the time, the NB complained of a 'secret agreement' between the 'Caley' and the LNWR to exchange traffic between each other. At that point, the stockholders must have realised that they were wasting their time!

Even when London (St. Pancras)-Edinburgh (Waverley) services became a daily commonplace, revenue was disappointing. At one time the NB was demanding compensation from the Midland for having to run so many unremunerative trains on the Waverley Route, particularly in winter. The demand was successful; £11,000 was handed over in the period. The NB's attitude seems more than a mite unfair; the Edinburgh company had never failed to urge the Midland to finish its Settle-Carlisle route in the 1870s. The latter company was also a generous partner in the consortium to build the Forth Bridge, its contribution greater than any other railway company's, including the NBR.

Acquiring the Port Carlisle Branch gave the company access into north-west Cumbria, and it seemed at one time as if the NBR would even be involved in backing the Solway Junction Railway, with its 1,900 yard viaduct across the estuary. Although we look back on the Solway Viaduct as carrying a Caledonian line, the North British were so interested in the SJR in the late 1860s that they opened negotiations with the new company about installing NBR staff at Annan Station (later Annan Shawhill), while Annan itself was listed in a parliamentary document in 1865 as an exchange point for traffic between the NBR and GSWR!

However, when the SJR directors began to experience financial difficulties – and early traffic returns were disappointing – the NBR was in something of a fiscal trough itself, and the Caledonian hurriedly stepped in, securing an agreement to work the Solway line from its opening in 1869. The NBR contented itself instead with its new acquisition of a branch to Silloth.

Was building the Waverley Route worth it? Probably not. Traffic receipts at main line Newcastleton were always inferior to those of branch line Langholm, and Anglo-Scottish services could not equal the timings of the East and West Coast rivals even when the latter two routes were slowed by the 1896 timing cartel. Freight traffic was reasonably heavy, although few of the cargoes were generated on the 40 miles or so of some of the dreariest, least fertile terrain imaginable on the British mainland.

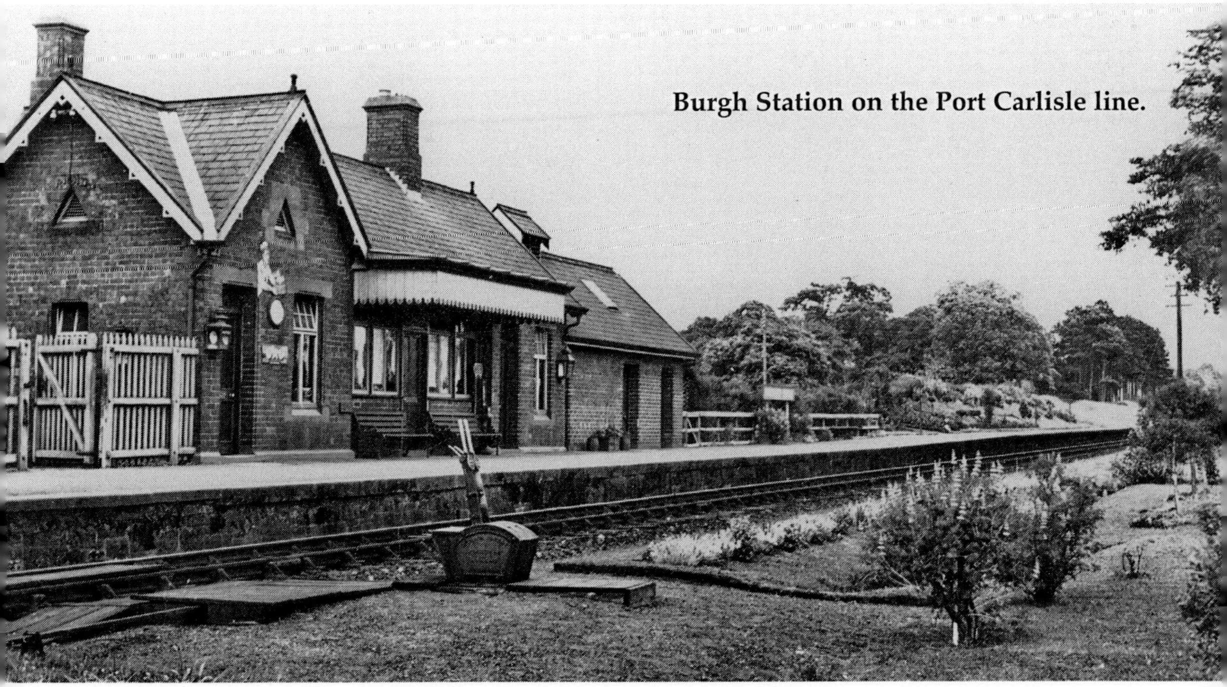

Burgh Station on the Port Carlisle line.

Bridging the Tay – Twice

Its takeover of the Edinburgh Perth & Dundee Railway in 1862 had established the North British in the "Wee Kingdom" of Fife – a county where it was soon to enjoy a monopoly. Of course, there was no question of there being an 'East Coast' route north of Edinburgh, as long as the firths of Forth and Tay remained unbridged.

In Scotland, a 'firth' is defined as 'an arm of the sea', and this sums up the problem facing the Edinburgh company. In addition to the usual challenge of bridging a river, a bridge over the sea demanded that maritime interests and agencies should be satisfied that fishing and shipping activities would be unaffected, and that the possible corrosive effects of salt water on metal be taken into account. The potential for stormy weather however, did not enter into Victorian thinking – such was the self-confidence of engineers and railway promoters in the mid-19th century.

In planning to bridge the Tay, the NBR was addressing itself to the lesser of the two challenging firths. Shipping and fishing interests upstream, including Perth Harbour, could be satisfied with a proposed viaduct some 70 feet above the water, and with no opening span, something which even the Solway Firth crossing appeared to require at one time. There would however, have to be a girder section higher than the rest of the structure to offer increased clearance over a ship's mast. The proposed site of the bridge had to be moved upstream from the company's first choice – from Tayport to Broughty Ferry – so as to leave the port of Dundee unimpeded. A record would be attained by the bridge's owners, for this would be the longest bridge in Britain, indeed Europe, at the time and for many years afterwards. Nevertheless, the logistics of this sea-crossing appeared manageable.

It was at this stage that the North British Railway made the first of its many mistakes in the sorry saga of bridging the Tay. The company appointed a certain Thomas Bouch as its engineer on the project, and this was to prove disastrous. Bouch had worked for the Edinburgh Perth & Dundee Railway (then the Edinburgh and Northern) in providing a

The North British pier at Broughty Ferry, the gantry for Bouch's bridge, that allowed loading of train ferries, is on the left below the level of the stone pier.

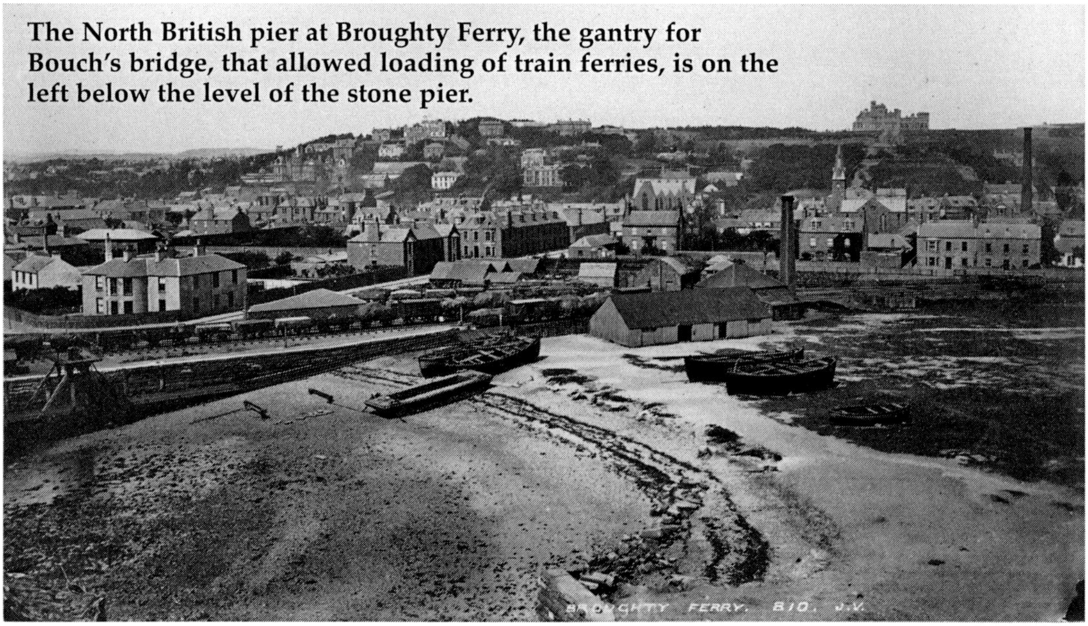

'flying bridge' at Granton and Burntisland, effectively a ramp loading arrangement to allow speedy loading and unloading of what turned out to be one of the world's first regular train ferries. He had gone on to design some impressive viaducts in the north of England – none more so than on the cross-Pennine line from Darlington to Tebay – but his record as engineer on a number of minor Scottish lines was less than impressive.

Nevertheless the NBR allowed Bouch to proceed with a design for a single-track viaduct, which, although graceful in appearance, led some local people to forbid their children ever to travel on it. Not only did it appear insubstantial, it had been poorly constructed by unsupervised contractors, as was soon to be revealed in the most horrific manner possible.

The bridge had been open for less than two years when Scotland was swept by a storm from the west which we would now call 'the storm of the century', as the media describes any wind of more than 80 mph. However, there was no exaggerating this meteorological holocaust on December 28th 1879.

An Edinburgh-Aberdeen train, whose doomed passengers had already had to endure a crossing of the Forth between Granton and Burntisland, arrived at Wormit, at the southern end of viaduct when the storm was at its height. Incredibly, railway managers were prepared to allow the express to proceed on to the bridge, and it was last seen steaming out into the dark heart of the storm. Its crew and passengers were never seen alive again.

The Tay Bridge Disaster must rank as one of the most preventable accidents of all time. It should have taken no imagination or indeed common sense for the train to be held on the Fife bank until the wind had lessened. What actually happened that night was of course the subject of a Board of Trade Inquiry, and continuing speculation ever since. What the inquiry established beyond all doubt was that the bridge had been badly constructed, with imperfectly-prepared metalwork being produced at the Wormit foundry, with no proper inspection procedures. Incredibly, Bouch had not taken wind speeds into account when designing the structure, and his nonchalant attitude was mirrored by the usual casual inspection by the Board of Trade.

It mattered little that Queen Victoria had been impressed by the bridge in 1878, and had knighted Bouch. The accident inquiry mercilessly reported that "the bridge was badly designed, badly constructed and badly maintained". The report blamed Bouch on all three points, although the NBR was certainly culpable for not having issued its staff with instructions about holding trains in bad weather. Bouch never survived this professional execution, dying later that year, less than 12 months after the tragedy. The work he was already undertaking in building a Forth Bridge – complete with towers 150 feet higher than those ultimately built – was mercifully halted.

If any good came out of this terrible incident, it was that engineers began to treat Nature's elements with more respect. It certainly woke up the Board of Trade to its responsibilities – its previous 'inspection' of the Leaderfoot Viaduct is referred to in the Waverley Route chapter, where a railway structure had to receive major emergency repairs within six months of being 'approved'. The Forth Bridge was to be subjected to no fewer than 28 inspections before opening, so clearly a lesson had been learned from the Tay incident.

A new Tay Bridge was begun in 1882 some 60 yards west of the old structure, whose piers can still be seen. The second bridge was opened in July 1887, but it was to be nearly another three years before an 'East Coast' railway from London to Aberdeen became a reality.

Locomotives to 1906

In the spring of 1845, the North British Railway took delivery of its first locomotives. They came by sea, delivered to the still-incomplete railway at Berwick-on-Tweed by the Newcastle firm of Hawthorn.

No fewer than 38 engines were ordered, comprising 0-4-2, 0-6-0, and 2-2-2 wheel arrangements. The latter two were for use on the Edinburgh and Dalkeith system, but as that was undergoing regauging, the engines concerned were likely to be part of the overall pool of motive power. It was a pool deeper than required, and a number of NBR locomotives began their working lives on loan to the bustling Edinburgh & Glasgow. Meanwhile, Hawthorn's were so impressed with the potential Scottish market that they quickly opened a factory at Leith to cope with demand.

So began the history of the NBR's locomotive fleet. Unlike the Caledonian, which leased neighbouring lines' engines from the start, the North British began with its own, if only because its newly-absorbed rival, the Edinburgh and Dalkeith, had no engines to offer (apart from a stationary unit at St. Leonard's), being literally horse-powered.

Not until the early 1870s did the North British locomotive policy really hit its stride. Engines were absorbed from the Edinburgh Perth & Dundee and Edinburgh & Glasgow in 1862 and 1865 respectively, with the latter bringing in more 'single-wheelers', where tractive effort was transferred to the rail by a single pair of drivers, often of great height.

The company's earliest locomotive works was situated on the up side of the line at St. Margaret's, close to where Meadowbank Stadium is now. The first locomotive superintendent was Robert Thornton, previously a Hawthorn's employee. History records

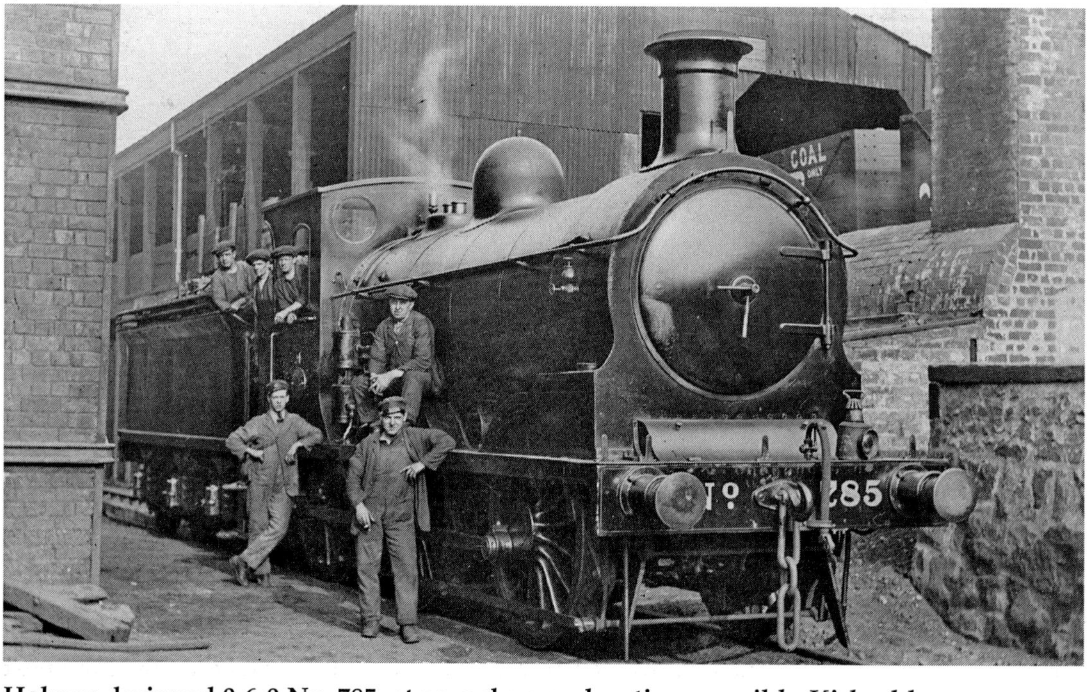

Holmes designed 0-6-0 No. 785, at an unknown location, possibly Kirkcaldy.

that he was so disgusted with the cheeseparing way the NBR attempted to keep its motive power in working order that he walked off the job. After two temporary appointments, William Hurst was next to try and keep the trains running, with, remarkably, no fewer than 22 engines actually being built on this site. After 1865, new construction and the heaviest repairs could be undertaken at Cowlairs in Glasgow, with St. Margaret's, and the newly-acquired Burntisland workshops, relegated to lighter repairs.

The succession of Hurst's successor Thomas Wheatley, by Dugald Drummond, ushered in a new era into NBR locomotive matters in 1875. Feared as much as he was respected, Drummond spent slightly less time with the company than he did with the Caledonian, but he established a tradition of building and operating inside-cylinder 4-4-0 passenger engines that not only served the NBR right up to Grouping in 1923, but was also taken up on three other Scottish lines and the London & South Western Railway. Strictly speaking, Wheatley had begun it all with his introduction of the two examples of the 224 class of 1871, with 224 herself having to be salvaged from the bottom of the Tay, thereafter running with the grim nickname of 'The Diver'. The North British owned no fewer than 183 4-4-0s when the company lost its independent identity in 1923, representing no less than one-fifth of the entire engine stud, both passenger and freight.

With Anglo-Scottish expresses expected to operate on the Waverley Route from 1876, Drummond built on Wheatley's foundations by designing a class of 4-4-0 known as the 476, or 'Abbotsford', class, named after Sir Walter Scott's Borders home. With driving wheels 78 inches in diameter, these were the most influential British locomotives of the decade, being described by contemporary railway author, Professor Foxwell, as achieving "the very best express running in the world over such hills'.

Just as Caledonian designers were to produce successive generations of inside-cylinder 4-4-0s over the decades from the drawing-boards of successive designers from Drummond to Pickersgill – and with an obvious debt to the 'Abbotsfords' – so the North British went on, under Holmes, Reid, and Chalmers, to produce its own 'generations' of compact, but powerful, 4-4-0s.

In the 15 years from 1884, Matthew Holmes, Drummond's successor, introduced three marques of 4-4-0, the '574', '633', and '729' variants, all of which were later rebuilt by W.P. Reid as Class 'M'. So sturdy were these machines that some survived to be taken into British Railways' stock in 1948. Later in the 1880s, Holmes produced another 4-4-0 design, known as 'West Highland Bogies', with 67 inch wheels, although they were less well-regarded on the Glasgow-Fort William route than later 4-4-0s built to operate it, namely the 'Glen' class, of which more later.

Holmes produced one more 4-4-0 strain, the unsuperheated '317' class in 1903, when other lines were already turning out much larger engines for their heaviest expresses. It was to be Holmes's last express engine, and not his best. His baton would be taken up by Reid, the Locomotive Foreman at St. Margaret's, who would continue the 4-4-0 tradition, but also introduce the Atlantic to NBR tracks.

The standard freight engine for the company was the inside-cylinder 0-6-0, from before the time the Berwick line opened, right up until Grouping in 1923. Indeed, the last NBR engines ever to operate in normal revenue-earning service, in 1967, were of this wheel-arrangement. Wheatley standardised the design from around 1867, turning out around 38 over the next eight years, but Drummond also produced them to an almost identical design. This resulted in the curious anomaly of members of the class being built new at the same time as their older siblings were being scrapped.

Undoubtedly the best-known 0-6-0 of the unsuperheated era was the C Class, designated as J36 after 1923. Known by this classification right into the 1960s, some of these engines achieved working lives of more than 70 years! Indeed, the last Scottish locomotive to be retired from normal service was, not an example of the BR 'Standard' building programme started in 1951, not a product of the LNER or LMS, not even one of Reid's new engines for the NB after 1906, but a Holmes 0-6-0! This was BR No. 65345, withdrawn from Thornton Depot on June 4th 1967.

Nor does the class need to be looked on as a forgotten product of the past, as one of these engines, No. 673 (BR 65243) is preserved in working order on the Bo'ness and Kinneil Railway. This carries the name *Maude*, not as in 'Come into the Garden …', but the name of a World War One general – no fewer than 25 of the class were shipped to the Continent during that conflict and worked on French railways. These were engines with a particularly interesting history, and we should be grateful that one has been preserved (and by enthusiasts, not by officialdom).

Another locomotive of that period which has survived to this day is the NBR Dock 'pug'. This was a type of shunting engine with a saddle tank over the boiler, and was usually attached to a wooden wagon to increase coal capacity. Later designated as Y9s by the LNER, these engines have been attributed to Dugald Drummond but were constructed by Neilson and Company. What is not in doubt was their longevity; one is preserved at Bo'ness. More than one chugged along Scotland's docksides for no fewer than 75 years, and they outlasted many of their larger stable-mates introduced 20 or 30 years later.

More modern units, the products of W.P. Reid, will be described later in this narrative.

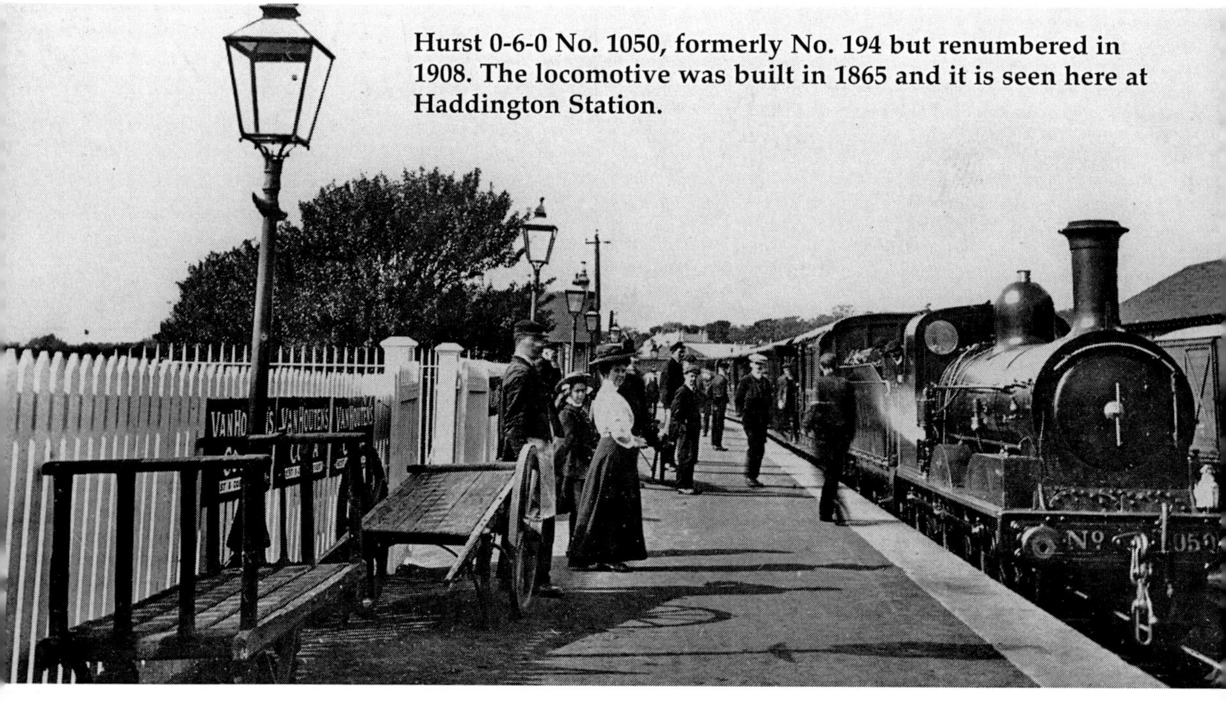

Hurst 0-6-0 No. 1050, formerly No. 194 but renumbered in 1908. The locomotive was built in 1865 and it is seen here at Haddington Station.

Travelling by Night

Night travel on railways was hardly a new idea in the 1870s, and had been an operational necessity in other, larger, countries, for many years. Curiously, it was the North British, a line not particularly noted for the quality of its passenger services, that was first to introduce a sleeping car in the UK, in 1873.

British rail journeys in the first 50 years of their history followed the pattern of travel made traditional by the stage coach and the foot traveller, from a time when nobody would dream of being on the road after dark, unless there was a full moon to provide illumination. Indeed, so unusual was the idea of night travel in the British Isles in the 18th century that the Birmingham Lunar Society, one of the nation's earliest intellectual groups, was so-called because of its timetabling of meetings to coincide with a full moon for its members to return home with some light to guide them.

Not only did the world's first railway passenger coaches resemble stage-coaches on rails, the custom of daylight journeys also transferred on to the railways. Anglo-Scottish travellers from the mid-19th century were offered a choice of "resting places", such as York or Peterborough, where they could break their journey overnight. The introduction of a sleeping carriage on to Britain's railway system failed to change all that, at least at first.

Looking back through the archives, the railway historian cannot help noticing that a number of railways involved in lengthy Anglo-Scottish services, appear to have hit on the idea of sleeping car services at around the same time in 1873. The North British started in April, its southern partner the Great Northern in July, the rival West Coast companies in October. This may have been more than a case of imitation being the most sincere form of flattery, as there is evidence of entrepreneurial activity in easing all these companies into the sleep-while-you-travel idea. It came from the Manchester firm of John Ashbury Ltd.

Ashbury's was a firm of carriage and wagon makers started by John Ashbury (1806-66) at Openshaw, Manchester in 1847, and was eventually to become, many years later, a constituent of the Metro-Cammell group. Its owner boasted that he produced a wagon in only thirteen hours for an exhibition in 1862, but he sold the firm in the same year. The NBR records indicate that a demonstration was arranged for both the North British and their arch-rivals, the Caledonian, at the same time. The Manchester-made coach must have impressed them.

Thirty feet long, the first British sleeping car was six-wheeled, and comprised two 1st class compartments on either side of a toilet compartment which occupied the width of the vehicle. Each sleeping compartment had a fold-away-type bed which doubled as a seat during daytime, although there was no skimping on the sleeping arrangements. Each of the three beds measured 75 inches in length when the seat was inverted and the bed brought from out of the recess in the upholstery. There was a luggage space at one end of the car and a 2nd class compartment – furnished with horsehair-stuffed benches – at the other. Presumably servants travelled in this compartment, although there was no door from it into the nearer sleeping compartment.

However, this description fails to do justice to the vehicle's appearance. Its interior was panelled with polished silver walnut, set off with ebony and gold mountings. The furnishings were described as being silver-plated, which seems difficult to envisage nowadays, and the floor was covered by deep-pile carpet laid on kamptulicon, a material made from cork and natural rubber, lauded for its sound deadening qualities. External panelling was teak, while the six four-foot diameter wheels had wooden centres with wrought-iron bosses and steel tyres.

Despite all this, *Engineering magazine* could only sneer at this "so called sleeping carriage", dismissing the Ashbury vehicle as 'simply a design based on the orthodox type of construction, extravagant in dead weight, and after all deficient in comfort or suitable arrangements'.

It seems churlish to criticise this pioneering sleeping car so severely. While its provision of seating converting into beds might seem to disqualify it as a dedicated sleeping car, the greater duration of Anglo-Scottish services in those days necessitated accommodation which would be equally suitable for the hours of daylight. At least *Engineering magazine* mentioned this innovation; the *Railway Times* was more concerned with a possible merger between the NBR and the Caledonian, which was mooted at the time.

Neither the public nor the working timetables of the NBR contain any mention of the new service, or its operational requirements, until October 1st 1873, when travellers were informed that the 'new NB sleeping carriage runs statedly from Glasgow Queen Street to London King's Cross every Monday, Wednesday, and Friday by Fast Train'.

This was the 9 pm out of Queen Street, restarting from Edinburgh Waverley at 10.30 pm. The coach returned on Tuesday, Thursday, and Saturday, as part of the 8.30 pm northwards from King's Cross, "extra charge Up or Down, 10s.", this in addition to the 1st class single fare of seventy shillings. Records show that an average of two passengers per journey made the trip in the weeks ending 17th and 24th of August, the average for six weeks up to September 21st being 2.3 passengers per journey.

Modest though it was, this was the beginning of a new era in British railway travelling!

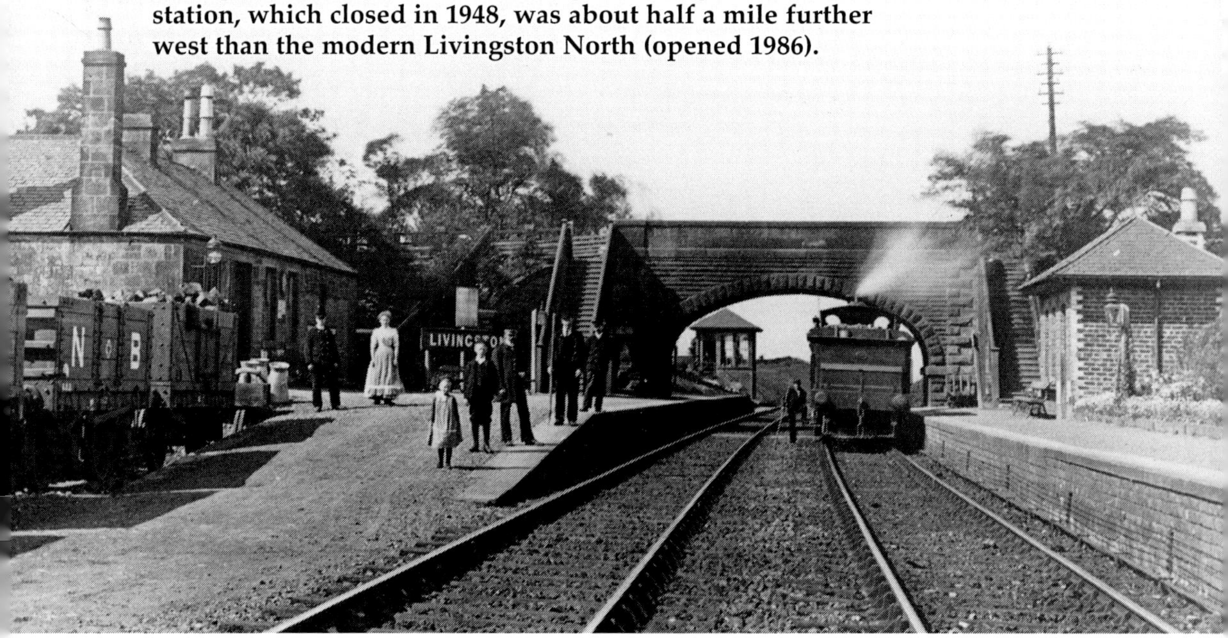

Livingston Station on the Edinburgh to Bathgate line. The station, which closed in 1948, was about half a mile further west than the modern Livingston North (opened 1986).

New Stations - Edinburgh

We have already seen that Edinburgh's Waverley Station was fast becoming a victim of its own success. By 1868, when the NBR transferred Fife and Aberdeen traffic from Canal Street into the main Waverley platforms, the situation became intolerable. Twenty years later, it was near-chaotic, and the company faced even greater traffic levels within two years when the Forth Bridge was expected to open. With the company committed to building approach lines to the bridge from north and south, the prospect of enlarging Waverley Station, and doubling its approaches through urban properties to east and west (including Princes Street gardens), must have seemed financially unsurmountable.

But in 1888 the NBR enjoyed a stroke of luck in their dealings with the hostile town council. While the latter was opposed to a doubling of lines through the Gardens, plus a new tunnel from Haymarket and a doubling of the Mound tunnels (actually two new single bores), a new threat to Edinburgh's amenities was proposed from a rival source. This was a Caledonian line running from beneath its Princes Street terminus, under the length of Princes Street itself, and then burrowing through the Calton Hill to a junction near Lochend, to meet with an over-ground line running across Leith from Trinity. If the NBR plans appeared unacceptable, the thought of trains (steam-hauled trains!) belching their smoke through vents in the middle of Princes Street, was the last straw for the council.

The North British was not slow to see an opportunity. By offering to build a short branch from Abbeyhill to the bottom of Leith Walk, the company challenged the 'Caley's claim that a Leith connection from that company was directly in the public's interest, thus buying off the city's objections to the doubling of lines in Princes Street Gardens.

As a result, the Caledonian lost its parliamentary application for a sub-Princes Street line, while the NBR received a green light to enlarge its facilities in the Waverley area. This would include the replacement of the North Bridge with a newer three-arch structure (which survives today). The only major price the company had to pay (in addition to the actual costs of improvements, costs which immediately started to pay for themselves) was a legal obligation to build and operate an Abbeyhill-Leith line.

The new Waverley was the biggest station in the UK at the time. Covering 23 acres, it comprised 21 platforms, two of them each catering for two through trains simultaneously; there were even two through platforms for suburban trains. In addition there were two dead-end termini configured back-to-back, the new layout being capable of simultaneously accommodating over 350 contemporary carriages if need be.

Between the wars, the LNER invested heavily in the Waverley, introducing track-circuiting and colour-light signalling, and converting one of the now-redundant manual boxes into a studio for (usually muffled) PA announcements. The station was considerably rationalized in the 1960s and 1980s, losing eight of its platforms, and with the old booking hall being cosmeticised out of existence. The magnificent wooden booking office was broken up, with the centre of the hall given over to catering. The corridor to eastbound trains was closed off (there are few eastbound trains anyway, compared to 1910).

Any stranger to the city looking at a map, would conclude that Waverley Station is perfectly positioned for the city centre. The Old Town is immediately to the south, the New Town and Princes Street cheek-by-jowl to the north. The reality is of course different.

Because Waverley is well below the level of both Princes Street and the Royal Mile, it requires arriving passengers to either climb out of it up heart-stopping ramps or steps, or join the lengthy taxi queue. Needless to say, neither means of gaining ground-level appeals to regular commuters – and their cause was not helped by the Suburban platforms being built on the 'wrong' side of the station, nearer the Old Town than the offices of the New. As a result, the limitations of the site have killed the city's suburban rail network, just as a local newspaper predicted as far back as 1925. The solution suggested then, escalators to take arriving passengers to street-level, did not materialise until 2011.

While the Waverley nowadays can hardly satisfy the modern commuter's expectations in terms of access and egress, it still plays an important part in the UK's long-distance transport network. Recent research shows that in 1910 the Waverley directly served no fewer than 186 stations within 15 route-miles; nowadays the number served within that distance barely breaks into double figures. Yet trains to London and Glasgow are far more frequent than they ever were. In other words, Waverley Station is a commuter's nightmare, but plays its part in the overall national network.

Meanwhile, Leith Central was the price the NBR had to pay for a free hand in rebuilding Waverley. The company delayed construction for as long as possible, until the town clerk of Leith started ominously to remind the NB of its legal obligations under the Waverley Station Extension Act of August 5th 1891. The result was a station for Leith designed without any reference to operational practice or public needs – a huge covered terminus, between Leith Walk and Easter Road, capable of handling main line trains in its four platforms and eight sidings. Destined to last only 50 years, the Central has now vanished from the urban landscape, a fascinating footnote in Edinburgh (and Leith's) transport story.

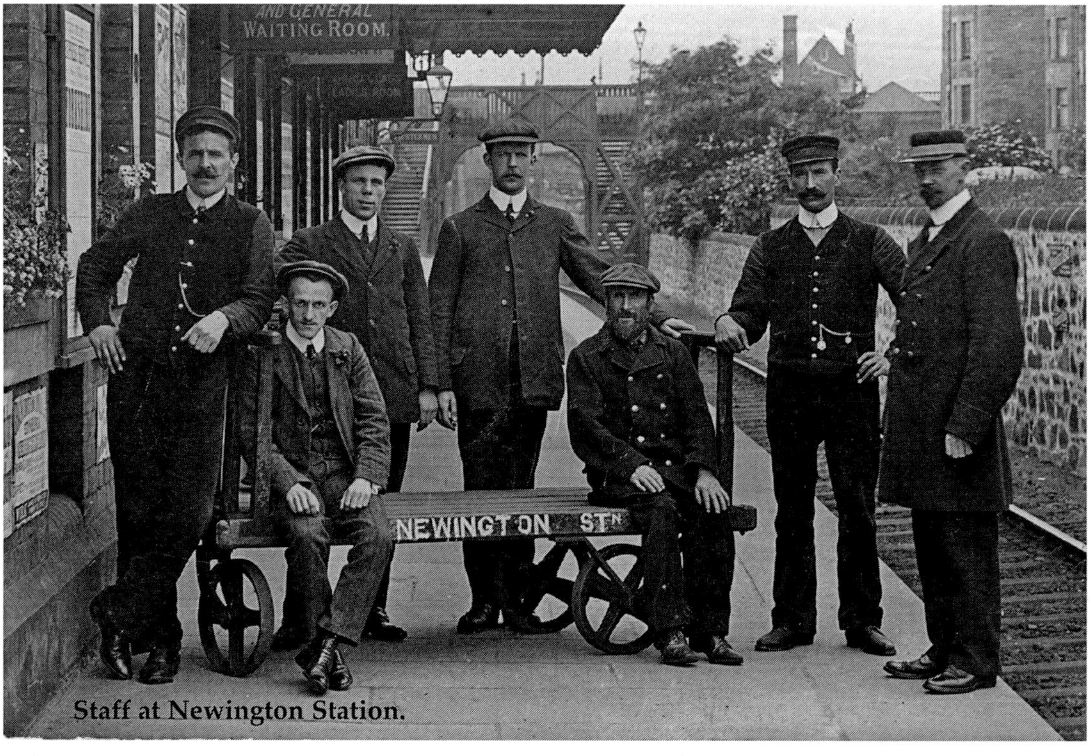

Staff at Newington Station.

Burrowing Under Glasgow

Although Glasgow might have been regarded as Caledonian territory, that company was pre-empted in the building of a cross-city underground line by both the NBR and the cable-operated Underground. In the form of the Glasgow City and District line, in 1886 the NBR ambitiously built at right angles under its Queen Street terminus and provided a passenger service along the north bank of the Clyde, linking Bellgrove – or farther afield to the east – with a link to the west as far as Loch Lomond. Effectively this was through a $2\frac{1}{2}$ mile tunnel, with Queen Street almost exactly half way along. Dynamiting could not be used in tunnelling, and geological conditions were endlessly challenging but the GCD pressed on, creating only the fourth 'underground' railway in the UK at that time.

Any first-time visitor to Queen Street main line station in the days of steam might be puzzled by its description as 'High Level', bearing in mind how trains have to descend into it through a tunnel of Stygian gloom. For there is a 'Low Level' station at right angles to its upper counterpart, and it has always been busier than its 'upstairs' equivalent.

Opened in 1886, this lower station originally comprised four platforms (lettered A-D, and not numbered until 1954), offering steam-hauled services to Helensburgh, Milngavie, and Balloch to the west, and Bellgrove, Airdrie, and even Edinburgh (Waverley) eastwards. At the outbreak of the First World War in 1914, there were no fewer than 165 trains each way daily through Low Level, but even as late as the 1950s, the steam locomotives operating the 98 daily trains each way added to the grime in the station. Because of its track configuration, effectively a double loop, services could overtake each other here; one evening train from Clydebank was scheduled to be passed by two other services at this time.

Electrified in 1959, the 'Low Level' station has had its platforms reduced to two, but there is still a good service selection in the westward direction, and through to Edinburgh after the Airdrie – Bathgate line was reopened on 8th March 2011.

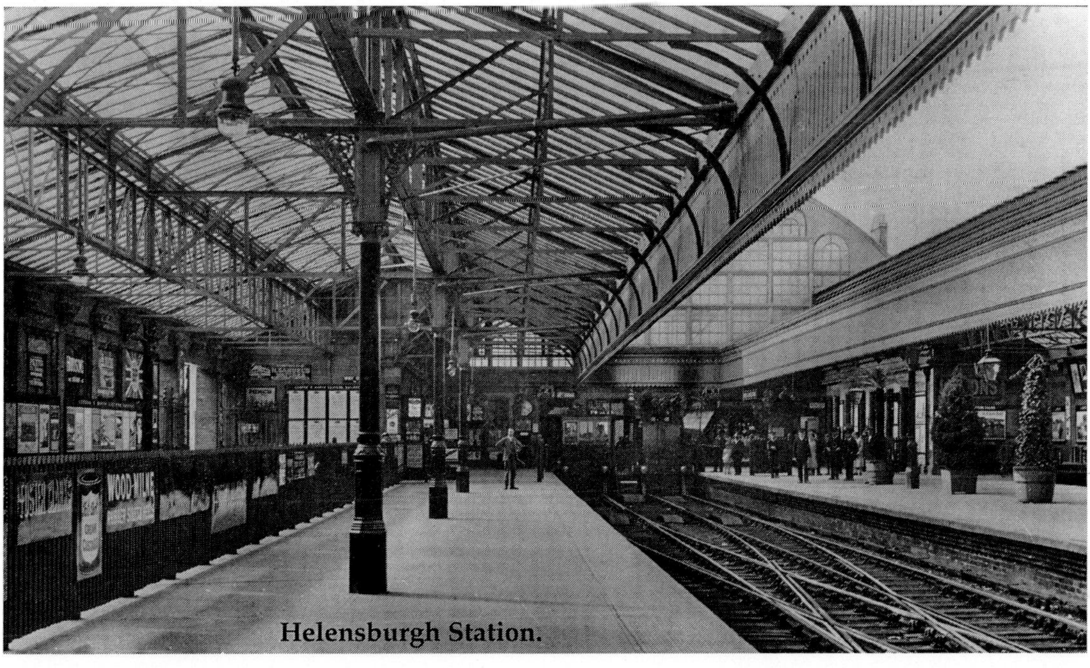

Helensburgh Station.

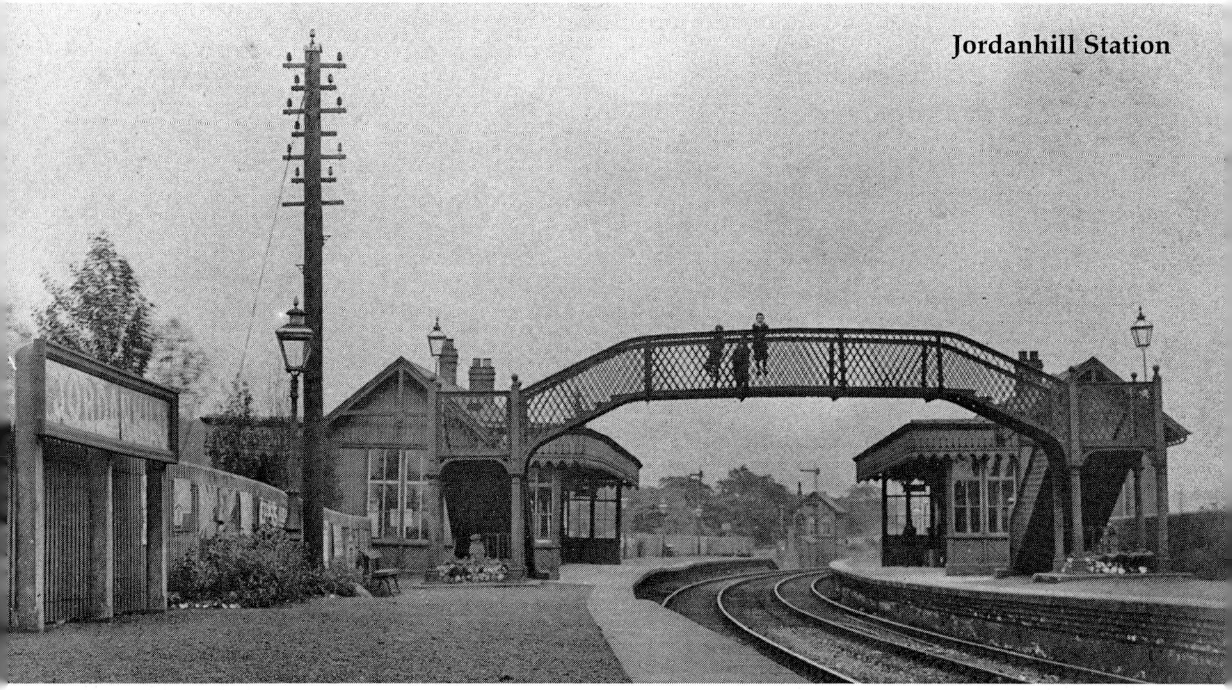

Jordanhill Station

The mainstay of steam-operated services through Low Level was the tank engine. When the line opened, Drummond and Holmes tank locomotives were seen here daily, mainly 0-4-4Ts of class P. Reid built no fewer than three passenger tank classes, one an 0-4-4T which the LNER classed as a G9 but which failed to establish itself on this part of the system, and two 4-4-2 classes, which certainly did. But the use of Hyndland as a terminus permitted through services to run from Hamilton and Edinburgh, and 4-4-0s were seen daily on these.

It was unthinkable that the Caledonian could not do as least as well, and the Glasgow Central Railway was opened ten years after the NB's, running from Rutherglen along the north bank of the Clyde, through a new low-level Central Station, to the Stobcross dock area and destinations even farther west. Curiously, this rival cross-Glasgow line succumbed to changed traffic demands, and closed in the 1960s – probably the public was simply fed up with the dirt and condensation of the underground stations. This line reopened in 1979, the local authorities realising that they needed all the transport arteries they could lay their hands on.

In contrast, the NBR system was electrified in 1959 (although steam had to make a belated return to service when the 'Blue Trains' had to be temporarily withdrawn for a ten-month period), but there has never been any question of the former-NBR link closing. The main criticism one could make of these Pressed Steel units, now withdrawn, was their livery – Caledonian blue was hardly appropriate for this line! Regular passengers might add that, if criticisms are being sought, the riding of these electric trains left much to be desired.

One reason for the former North British line being more popular than its Caledonian counterpart in the days of steam (or perhaps less unpopular) was that locomotive exhaust could escape more easily from Queen Street (Low Level) than from the Central underground line. The latter was truly in tunnel, whereas both the 'subterrestrial' stations at Queen Street and Charing Cross allowed some measure of ventilation.

Bridging the Forth

If the Firth of Tay was an engineering challenge for the North British, requiring two entirely different bridges, and costing 75 passengers' lives, the Firth of Forth was something else again.

At least the Tay, with only light river traffic, and no nearby naval base, could be bridged at a height of no more than 70 feet. But the traditional crossing point on the Forth at Queensferry was downstream from the new naval base, and the Admiralty was not slow to inform the NBR that a clearance of 150 feet would be required at high tide, in order to let the largest battleships to pass. Nor could a tunnel be contemplated, with two underwater channels going as deep as 200 feet at this point. Bridging the Forth was going to be an engineering challenge unlike anything ever seen before in the British Isles.

The NBR was quick to take the problem to its southern allies – the Great Northern and North Eastern on the East Coast, plus the Midland, which was planning to exchange cross-Border traffic with the NB at Carlisle within a few years. A consortium called the Forth Bridge Railway (FBR) Company was set up in 1873, getting off to an unfortunate start when its first board meeting had to be abandoned as inquorate.

Another unfortunate augury was the appointment as Sir Thomas Bouch as project engineer, who announced plans for a gargantuan suspension bridge, with supporting towers no less than 500 feet high from which gigantic tubes would be suspended on chains. The tubes, one hundred feet apart, would each contain a single line of track. Work began in 1878 with foundations being dug for one of the towers on Inchgarvie Island, in the middle of the traditional Queensferry passage.

The terrible storm of December 1879 did more than destroy Bouch's Tay Bridge; it destroyed its designer's reputation. Within eight months the FBR was asking Bouch if he would like to be relieved of his contractual obligations to them, while all work on the Forth was stopped, although not quickly enough to prevent the forging of the giant chains, for which Messrs Vickers had to be paid. Bouch demanded compensation for having his contract cancelled – was refused – and was dead within the year. The FBR cancelled its plans to bridge the Forth for the foreseeable future.

But the English participants in the consortium – not so directly affected by the Tay tragedy – were made of sterner stuff, and demanded that the matter be reconsidered. This was done at a meeting in York in January 1881, the outcome of which was that the three English companies secured representation on the FBR board, along with the appointment of two renowned engineers, Sir John Fowler and Benjamin Baker.

Fowler and Baker soon devised a cantilever design, based on traditional principals, and giving massive strength to what was basically a seamed viaduct running through the middle of the structure. The designers' philosophy was that "the successful engineer is he who makes the fewest mistakes". Their design was sound, and with Sir William Arrol contributing the steel, the engineering was equally good. It had to be, as the Board of Trade, notoriously casual in its approval of bridges and railways hitherto, now insisted on a quarterly inspection of the works. There were to be no fewer than 28 such inspections.

The bridge took seven years to complete, being opened in March 1890 by the then Prince of Wales (later Edward VII). The NBR now had an advantage of 29 miles over the Caledonian in operating Edinburgh-Aberdeen services, and 21 between Edinburgh and Perth. It had cost some 57 lives, and continued to incur casualties even after opening. It meant the closure of the Granton-Burntisland ferry to rail vehicles, although passengers were still making that crossing, in the absence of a road bridge, well into the second half of the 20th century.

Of course, this did not come cheaply to the NB, the Edinburgh company being responsible for the construction of approach lines to both north and south, including a seven-mile line from Burntisland to Inverkeithing as well as completing a spur connecting Dalmeny, on the south bank, with Winchburgh on the Edinburgh-Glasgow line, and thus allowing through traffic between Glasgow and Dundee and Fife. There was also the not-so-minor matter of having to rebuild Waverley Station, double its approaches, and construct an entirely new terminus in Leith. At least the NBR was able to recoup some of its investment; on opening, it charged the FBR £172 to hire two test trains weighing a total of 1,800 tons!

The North British's contribution to the FBR consortium was 30%, the Midland paying 32.5% and the GNR and NER, 18.75% each. Interestingly, the NBR was not the only company with running powers. While the Midland, like the other two English companies, held running powers over the Bridge, there is no record of such an arrangement on the Waverley Route, thus rendering the Midland's bridge powers purely academic. Not so with the North Eastern Railway, which was already operating Anglo-Scottish expresses north of Berwick, and could theoretically proceed even farther. At one time, when NER/NBR relations were at a low ebb over the vexed question of which company would power trains between Edinburgh and Berwick, the NER turned up the heat on its Edinburgh "ally" by demanding technical clearance to operate trains to Glasgow and Perth, as it was entitled to do! In contrast, the Midland's contribution was extremely generous considering the disappointing receipts on Waverley Route traffic.

To bring the story of the bridge up to date, we find that its history reflects that of the British railway system. In 1923 the FBR was not 'grouped' into any of the 'Big Four' companies, the LNER appointing six directors, with two from the rival LMS and two from the stockholders. In 1948 the company, and its sole asset, were nationalised, British Railways then realising that company law relating to the distribution of directorships had not been observed – the Forth Bridge was apparently administered illegally until 1948!

The bridge, after the railways were privatised in the mid 1990s, was a frequent target for media criticism as the traditional maintenance programme of 'three years of painting and then start all over again' could no longer to be observed. New safety legislation made maintenance much more difficult to accomplish in such dangerous conditions. In 2002 work began to restore the entire bridge and reduce the need for maintenance. This involved stripping all the accumulated layers of paint back to the steel so that repairs could be made. Then using modern paints designed to protect oil rigs the bridge was repainted in a coat that should last twenty years. Then only the top coat need be reapplied to continue to protect the bridge.

Described by one railway historian as 'having an unconscious beauty', the Forth Rail Bridge is still the most impressive man-made view in Scotland, if not the United Kingdom. A survivor of Luftwaffe bombing, and of the worst winds the North Sea can throw at it, the Forth Bridge is a credit to the railway companies who overcame their differences, pooled their resources, engaged two brilliant designers, a superb engineering contractor, and built Britain's finest man-made structure. In setting up the Forth Bridge Railway Company they also created probably the world's only railway company that owned launches (for inspection and rescue purposes), but no trains!

Locomotives 1906-22

William Paton Reid was the designer of those NBR engines which older railway enthusiasts still recall today. While best remembered for his Atlantics, it should not be forgotten that he also introduced three 4-4-0 designs, two of which were highly regarded by railwaymen over some 40 years, while his 0-6-0s were still working into the second half of the 1960s. His tank locomotives were no less interesting.

Reid's reputation as a locomotive designer pales in comparison with such Caledonian contemporaries as McIntosh and Pickersgill, and he seems to have enjoyed little eminence within his own organisation, at least to begin with. This was possibly because his appointment was the product of board infighting in 1903, with Reid being promoted from a post at St. Margaret's.

When Reid's Atlantics first began operating in 1906, their designer had lost his boardroom patrons, and NBR directors hesitated not one moment to bring in eminent mechanical engineers from outside the system – Messrs Ivatt and Raven from allied railways on the East Coast Route – to assess their own engineer's workmanship. This was despite the fact that Reid's engines were perfectly satisfactory performers from the start; indeed Ivatt and Raven's recommendations for (purely detailed) 'improvements' do not appear to have required implementation.

Reid was entirely a prophet without honour in his own company, yet he was wise enough to build on the solid foundations of 4-4-0s and 0-6-0s produced since Wheatley's day. Many of these he rebuilt economically with superheaters and more humane footplate conditions for the crews, while at the same time building larger versions, culminating with the Atlantic class. Yet, as early as 1910, the Earl of Dalkeith, NBR chairman, told a meeting of stockholders 'We have no intention of building any more Atlantics'. This was the year before six more were ordered, with two more following in 1921, so the board showed their trust in Reid, in deed if not in word.

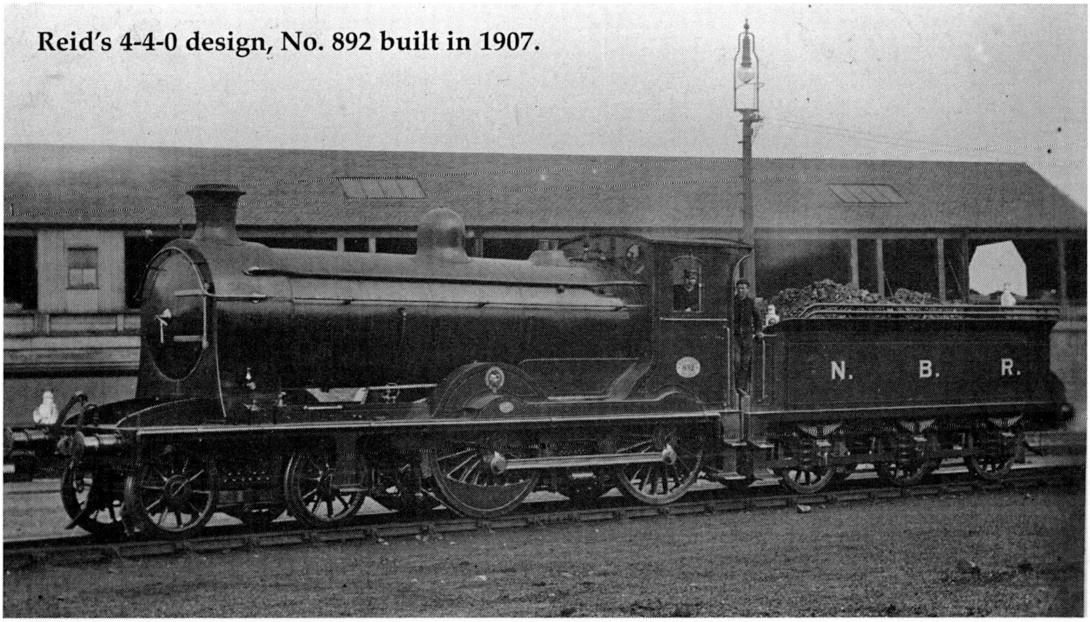

Reid's 4-4-0 design, No. 892 built in 1907.

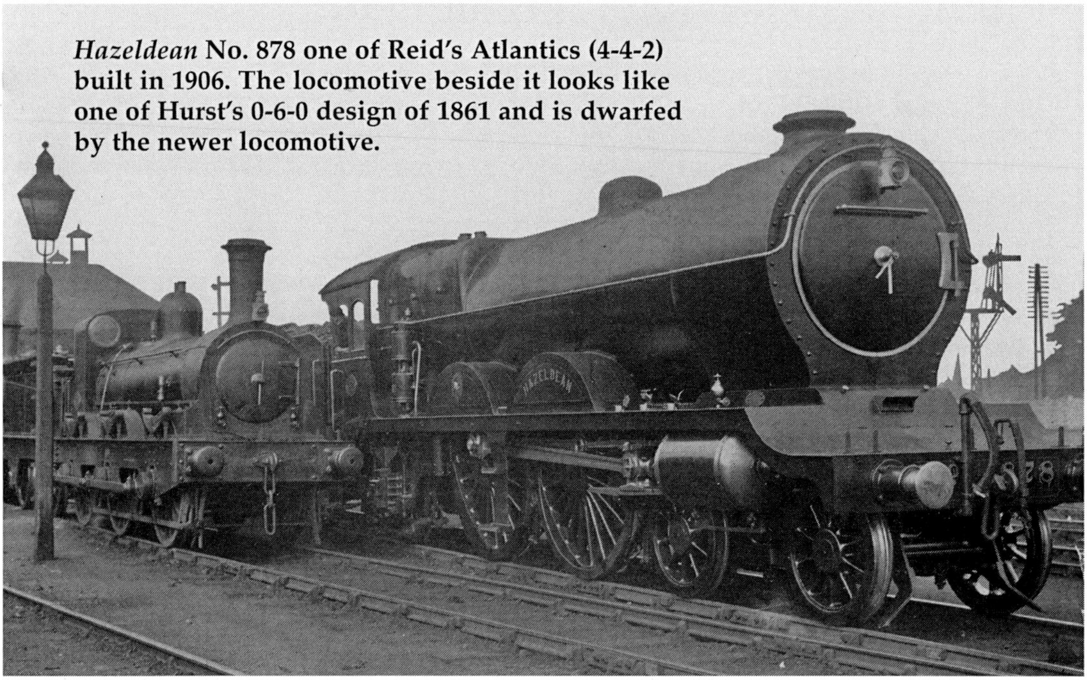

***Hazeldean* No. 878 one of Reid's Atlantics (4-4-2) built in 1906. The locomotive beside it looks like one of Hurst's 0-6-0 design of 1861 and is dwarfed by the newer locomotive.**

The first of his 4-4-0 locomotives comprised the 'Intermediate' class of 4-4-0. Introduced in 1906, these were mixed-traffic engines which were found almost everywhere on the system, equally at home on passenger or freight. Superheated in later versions of the class (D32 after 1923), some of its members survived until 1951.

Next came the 'Scotts', built first in a saturated version, then in superheated form. With larger driving wheels, these engines tended to be used most on the Edinburgh-Glasgow line, although they graduated down to branch line work later in their careers, which, like all Reid products, took them comfortably into their forties. While not invariably popular with their crews – they could be rough to ride – they carried some of the most striking names (from Scott again) of any British railway engines. Imagine if your train was hauled by a double-header of NBR nos. 421 and 499 – *Jingling Geordie* and *Wandering Willie*!

The last North British 4-4-0, and arguably the best of the lot, was the 'Glen' class. Introduced in 1913, and superheated from the start, these engines combined a good boiler and 72 inch driving wheels – six inches less than the 'Scotts'. The first members of the class went straight to the West Highland line, where the RCTS history of the class comments that "none of their six-coupled successors stood up to the pounding required on this severely-graded and awkwardly-curved stretch of line as well as they did". Later class members found employment all over the system and some were still working in the early 1960s. One of the class, No. 256 *Glen Douglas* is thankfully preserved.

Reid's best-remembered design – if not quite his masterpiece – was the 1906 class of Atlantics. These were massive looking engines, with their large boiler enforcing the use of a squat chimney and dome, and a Belpaire firebox (new to the NBR) emphasizing the appearance of great power. When railway author C. Hamilton Ellis first saw Atlantic No. 906 *Teribus* at Carlisle, he wrote that "to strangers, the name had a fine, if incomprehensibly terrific sound, entirely suitable to a large engine rushing through imposing scenery".

The railway industry at the time was surprised that the NBR had not aimed to rival the Caledonian's famous 4-6-0 designs, and retrospective criticism could be aimed at Reid for choosing the lesser adhesion of four powered wheels as opposed to six, as well as a high resulting axle load. At least Reid was, perhaps unconsciously, aligning himself with the express loco policy of East Coast allies, the Great Northern and North Eastern, and, interestingly, his Atlantics later acquitted themselves well against their southern rivals in LNER tests.

Yet a number of railway historians – particularly Cecil J. Allen – have had nothing good to say about *Aberdonian* and her sisters, presumably on the grounds of high coal consumption. This is a somewhat unreliable index on which to judge any steam engine, as no two crews would extract the same performance from a machine dependent on human muscle for fuel injection, or on skill, accumulated over many years, for driving performance. The fact that Reid's Atlantics were still operating express services on the East Coast line – particularly north of Dundee – into the mid-1930s, in competition with some of the finest designs of Sir Nigel Gresley – is final proof that William Paton Reid built his express engines to last!

That applied equally to his goods engines. The C class 0-6-0 designed by Holmes was the longest-serving NBR engine, but Reid built two classes which were equally reliable. His 'B' class of 1906 was followed by the superheated 'S' of 1914, both carrying boilers similar to the 4-4-0s being built at the same time. These 0-6-0s comprised the LNER J35 and J37 classes respectively. The 'S' was the most powerful freight engine built for the NBR, and the 104 members of the class could be found shunting the local yard, or heading freights across the Border all the way to Newcastle via Riccarton. While the Caledonian built 0-8-0s for its mineral traffic, the NBR contented itself with this class, the result of a gradual evolution of locomotive design which had begun in the 1840s, and able to negotiate all but the very worst rail conditions likely to be found in any siding or byway of the system.

Reid's earliest tank engine designs failed to rival his tender-engines for longevity. In 1909 he rather surprisingly perpetuated the 0-4-4T design begun by Holmes, quickly abandoning this for an Atlantic configuration. This comprised two tank locomotive designs for commuter and branch line work, the L and M 4-4-2 classes. One was basically a superheated version of the other, some of the earlier class being known as 'Yorkies', following a somewhat surprising decision to commission their construction from a Sheffield company. Although attractive in appearance, the C15 and C16s, as designated by the LNER, were replaced fairly quickly by a Gresley-designed tank locomotive, and failed to rival Reid's tender engines for long service.

For banking trains out of Glasgow Queen Street Station – it was decided to dispense with rope assistance in 1908 – Reid designed an 0-6-2 tank locomotive of considerable power. These were so successful that around 100 of these units were constructed, later being designated as Classes N14 and N15 by the LNER. They could be found all over the system, surviving into the early 1960s.

Curiously, when a Scottish enthusiasts' group balloted its members in the early 1960s about purchasing one for preservation, they received a very negative response. One can only speculate that, so common were these engines in yards up and down Scotland, that familiarity had bred contempt, and the society's members must wish now that they could have a second chance to buy a N15!

The NBR's last locomotive designer was Walter Chalmers, a draughtsman who had little time, in his three years of his appointment, or indeed little financial backing, to undertake

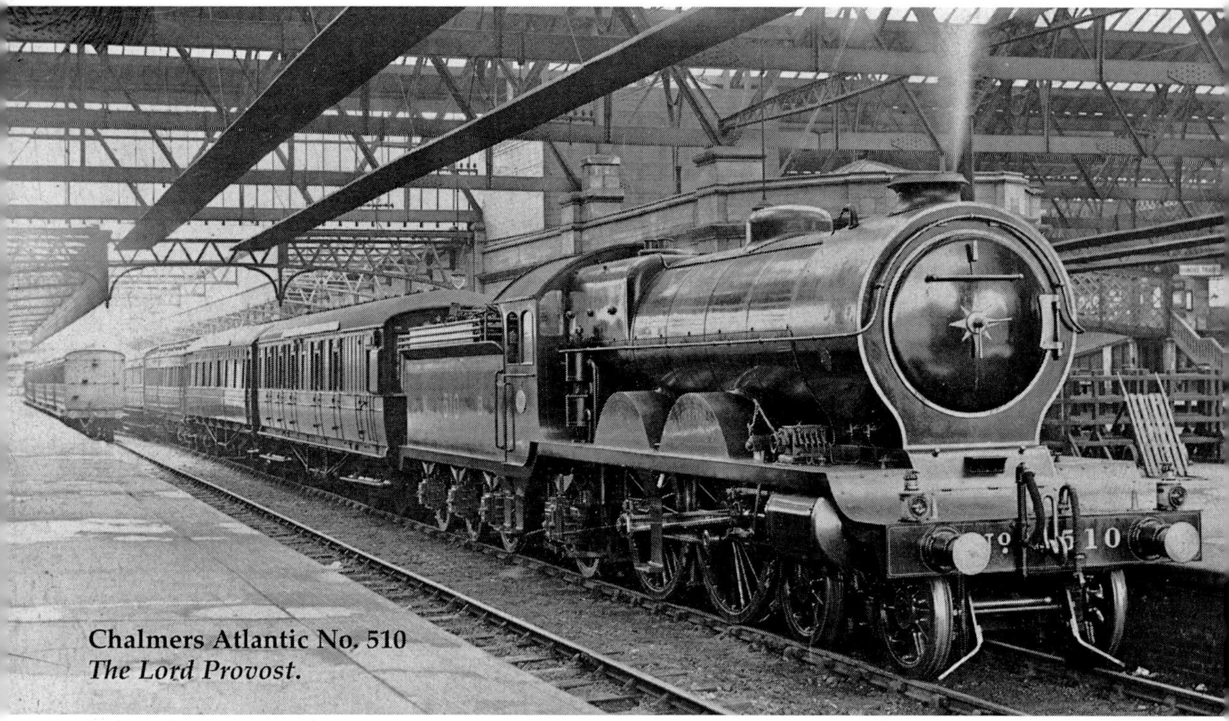

Chalmers Atlantic No. 510
The Lord Provost.

any design work. His main contribution seems to have been routine, in continuing Reid's highly economical policy of rebuilding Holmes's excellent machines, and in particular fitting them with cabs more in line with contemporary working conditions.

Chalmers was the one and only Chief Mechanical Engineer the NBR ever appointed; with J.P. Grassick taking over as Locomotive Running Superintendent, Reid's old job was effectively split in two. Reid had undertaken two men's work, and missed not one day because of illness in 16 years' service. The North British certainly had their money's-worth out of William Paton Reid.

The subject of locomotives should not be left without some mention of the unusual livery chosen by the NBR for its passenger engines. This was known as 'gamboge', perhaps best described as olive-green. Historian Hamilton Ellis believed that this shade was created by William Stroudley when he was briefly associated with the NBR through its takeover of the Edinburgh & Glasgow. Stroudley is best remembered for his express engines on the London Brighton and South Coast Railway, curiously lacking an unpowered front bogie or pony truck. These were painted yellow, although Stroudley claimed that they were green. Ellis believes that Stroudley was actually colour-blind, and that the condition had become worse by the time he took up a controlling position in locomotive affairs at Brighton.

In other words, the North British may have allowed a colour-blind engineer to suggest its locomotive livery! When the young Master Ellis told his mother that a NBR engine they had just seen was *gamboge* in colour, she took him to have his eyes tested!. It would be reasonable to say that the North British livery was less distinctive than the Caledonian's characteristic blue, although admirers of the company would be unable to imagine a Reid Atlantic in any other colour than – whatever it was!

Lothian Lines

As Glasgow flourished in the late 19th century, the North British Railway found it necessary to increase its passenger-carrying capacity by opening the City and District Line under the streets. In the Edinburgh area, however, it was not the passenger who made greater demands on the network – but coal.

Coal output from Mid and East Lothian collieries burgeoned towards the 2 million ton mark annually at the turn of the century, a large proportion being consigned for export. By 1913 even this total had doubled to more than 4 million tons, according to figures produced by the colliery owners, with no less than 70% being exported through Leith although these figures may have been inflated by the coal lobby to make its case to the NBR for better facilities.

Transshipment through Leith could only be done with some difficulty, as the rail approach to the port was down a 1 in 69 single-track incline (only doubled in the mid-1870s) from Portobello through Baileyfield and Seafield. Mineral wagons were hand-braked (even into the 1960s!), and had to have their brakes pinned down manually in descending such a hill, while travel in the other direction, even with empty vehicles, often required banking. All this lengthened each train's occupancy of the section.

Part of this line was the legacy of the Edinburgh & Dalkeith branch to Leith, and the NBR must have wished that they had persevered with its search for an alternative route to the port, something the directors instructed constructing engineer John Miller to survey as early as the

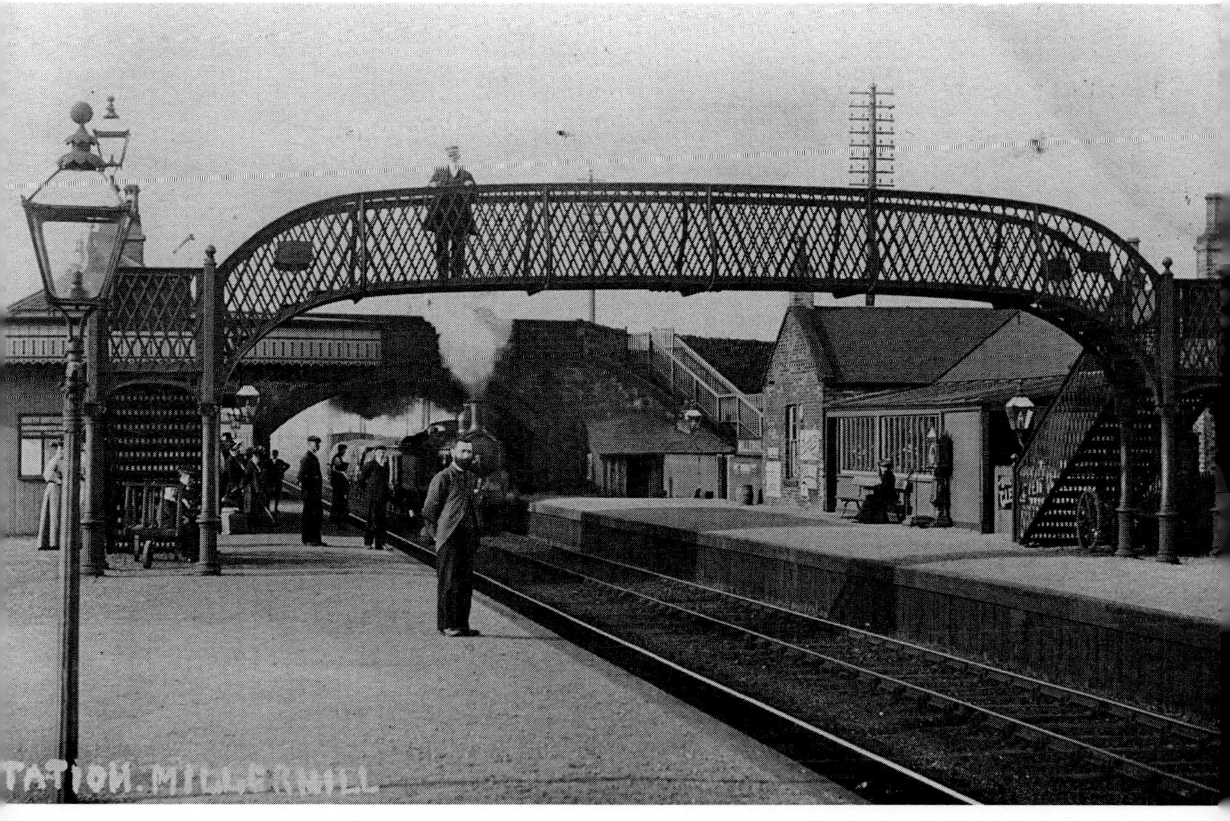

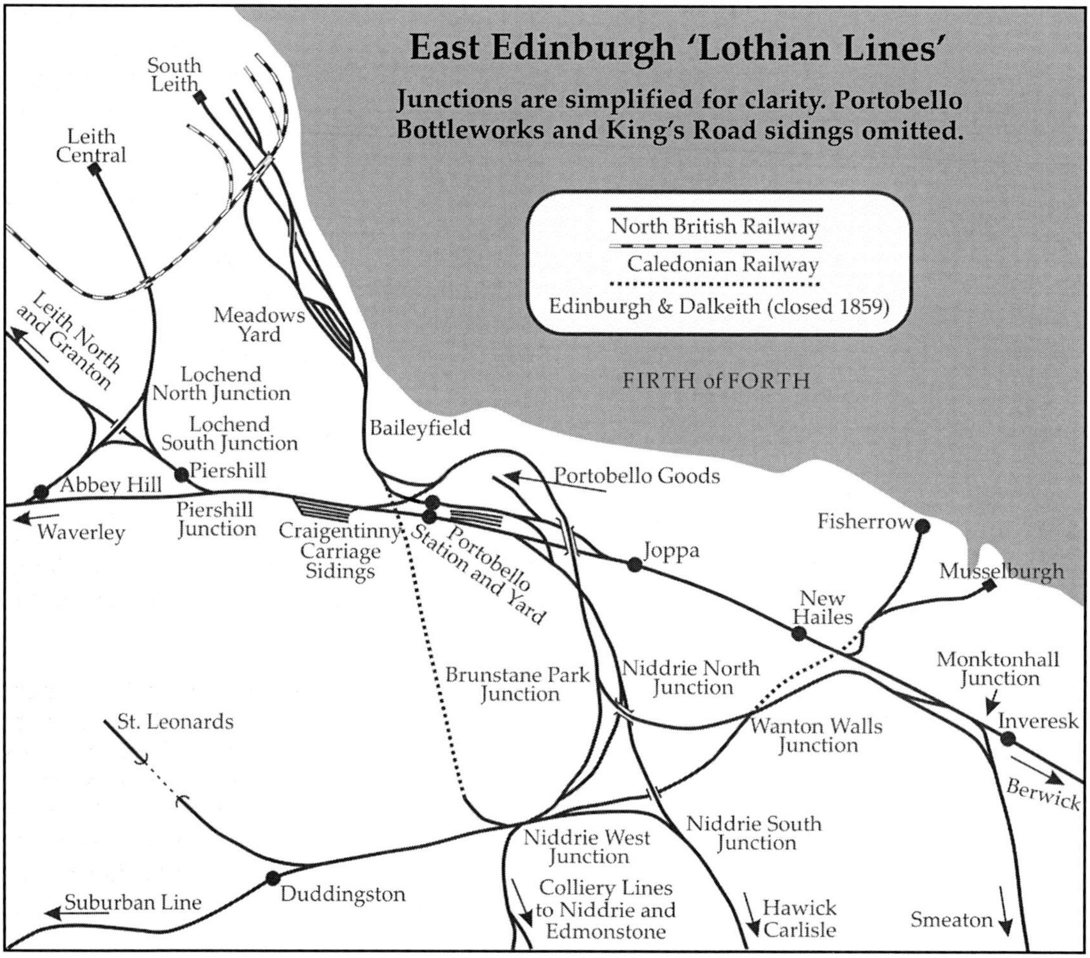

mid-1840s, before settling for modifying what they had received from the E & D. The latter reached Leith from Niddrie through Seafield. This Niddrie section was abandoned by the NBR and a connection made between Seafield and Portobello instead. Even the takeover of the Edinburgh Perth & Dundee in 1862 failed to alleviate the problem, since their Leith Citadel branch only allowed admittance to the docks over the busy thoroughfare of Commercial Street.

The Lothian coalmasters were not slow to complain about the NBR's service, pointing out that their Fife rivals could move coal to the quayside for a fraction of what the Lothian owners were paying. Of course, this was a benefit handed down from the Fife mine owners building their own waggonways to the Forth, as at Fordell and Charlestown – a history lesson not lost on the Lothian owners. In 1912, in the face of the NBR's continuing failure to modernise its Leith connection, the colliery companies decided to build their own railway!

In 1912 the Lothian Railways Bill was presented to Parliament, proposing a new eastern approach to the Edinburgh Dock at Leith. The route would have twice crossed that of the NBR, and also required an embankment in the sea! The NBR responded by trying to weaken the mining alliance by offering special terms to one or two individual companies, and the bill failed at Westminster. Nevertheless, as a bargaining counter, it was highly effective, and the NBR finally conceded that it would have to rebuild its approaches to the port.

The resulting network was known as the Lothian Lines, opening for business in September 1915. It involved improving the line down from Portobello, although with no alleviation of gradient, and a spur being put in, connecting with the new Caledonian lines on the east of the port (and allowing the NBR to lease the rival company's new locomotive depot known as Seafield).

But the main component of the new network was a single-line spur, operated under special signalling conditions, from the Leith line's junction at Portobello, climbing over the East Coast and Waverley Lines to a new high-level junction known as Niddrie North. From here, one line went on to join an extension from the Suburban Circle at Wanton Walls, and then rejoin the East Coast line at Monktonhall. Another met the Waverley Route at Niddrie South just before the present approach lines to the Millerhill 'hump', while the third spur headed west to join the Suburban Circle at Niddrie West.

So skillfully did this new system overlap existing lines that the single line over Portobello could carry coal traffic from Tranent, Macmerry, Newtongrange, Polton, Penicuik, Loanhead (and later Bilston), as well as Niddrie and areas north and west of Edinburgh via the Circle. It also had value as a diversionary route, and Deltic-hauled expresses were seen on it before the Niddrie-Portobello spur was closed in 1967. It was scarcely popular with 'Porty' residents; unfortunately, the sound of J35s, J36s, J37s and J38s pounding up the grade could go on all night!

The story of the Lothian Lines is an important one in the history of the NBR, as it shows the company having to address the dissatisfaction of customers who were simply too important to ignore. It also spurred the company to introduce Scotland's first Control Centre in 1913, facilitating the running of trains on the existing system, plus the assimilation of coal traffic on the new lines. The centre initially utilised the then newly-closed passenger building at Portobello, formerly serving the Leith branch, but the Control Centre was moved to Waverley within three years. Later Control Centres were established at Coatbridge for the west of the NBR system, and Burntisland, for the north.

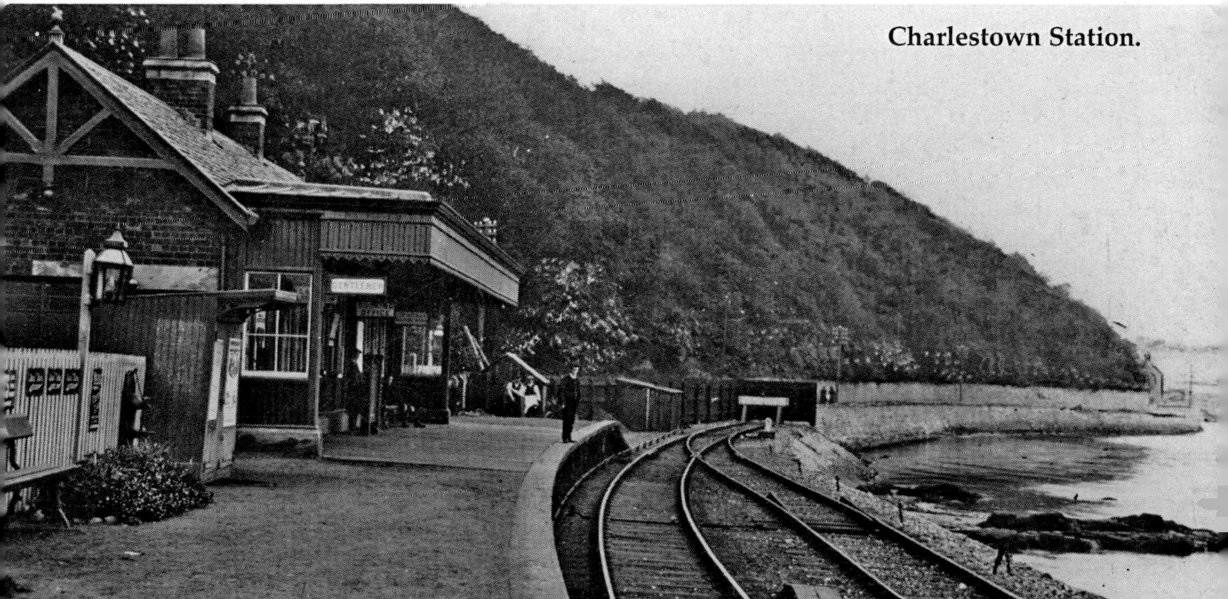

Charlestown Station.

To the West Highlands

In these days of railway closures and rationalisation, it is perhaps surprising that there are no fewer than three lines running to Scotland's north-west coast, all of them crossing harsh and sparsely-inhabited Highland landscapes.

The Caledonian penetrated to the Atlantic in 1880 through its constituent partner the Callendar and Oban line. The Highland Railway had already forged westwards from Dingwall, reaching Strome Ferry in 1870 and Kyle of Lochalsh some 27 years later. But Fort William was inaccessible by rail when these lines were being constructed, and local residents had long agitated for a railway connection.

The first proposal to receive Parliamentary examination came from a concern calling itself the Glasgow & North Western Railway, which proposed leaving the North British network immediately north-west of Glasgow, fringing Loch Lomond on its eastern side and, after crossing the Moor of Rannoch, descending through Glencoe to reach the coast. Not only would this have provided a southern approach into Fort William, but the promoters envisaged turning up the Great Glen from here and heading for Inverness. This really put the fat in the fire, ensuring opposition from three railways – from the North British, which felt its own approach to Loch Lomond might be compromised, from the Caledonian who reasonably felt that it should be allowed to approach Fort William from the Ballachulish area, and most of all from the Highland, which jealously fought to maintain its then monopoly in the Highland capital, Inverness.

The outcome was that the proposal was defeated by the weight of vested interests. Looking back, it seems obvious that no railway to Fort William could be tolerated by the Highland Railway unless an approach to Inverness was omitted from the prospectus, and in the late 1880s this is precisely how a local Fort William initiative laid the foundations for the present-day West Highland Railway.

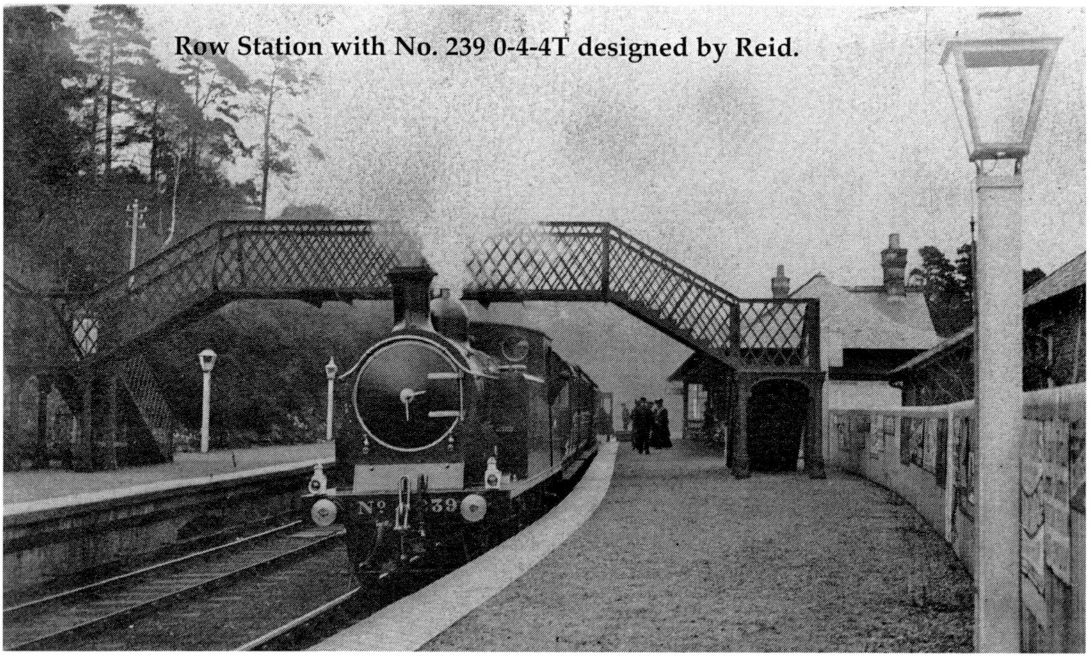

Row Station with No. 239 0-4-4T designed by Reid.

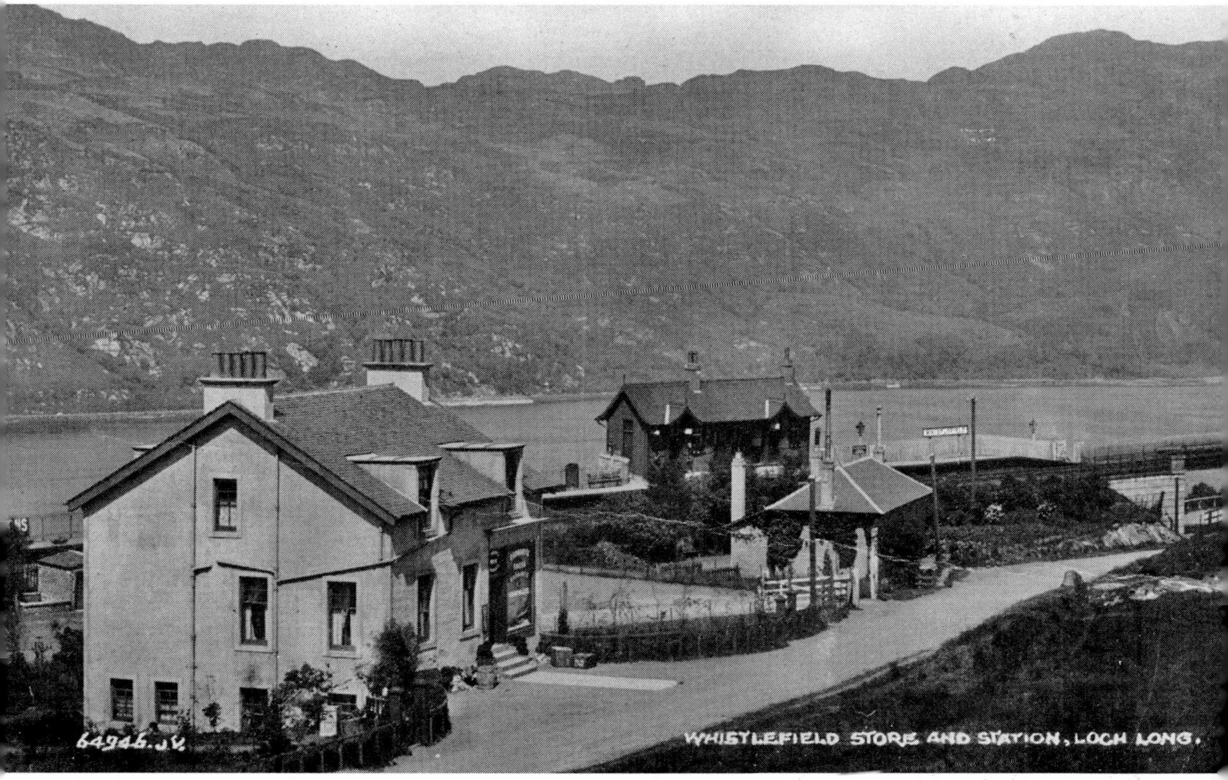

Travellers on the thrice-weekly coach to Kingussie began to question why this slow overland route was their only inland link with the south so late in the Railway Age, and in 1889 a company was formed with the sole purpose of connecting Fort William to the rail network. The omission of any declaration about reaching Inverness was crucial. On the one hand it diminished the line's prospects in the eyes of the Caledonian who were just down the coast at Oban (and who declined to consider operating it), but made the North British realise that a railhead could be established in the area without incurring the Highland Railway's wrath. The scheme envisaged the new line leaving the existing NBR network on the north side of the Clyde at Craigendoran, and striking up the Gareloch, Loch Long, and Loch Lomond, unlike the proposed Glasgow & North Western which would have traversed the eastern side of the 'Bonnie Banks'.

The perpetuation of the story about frustrated travellers on the Kingussie diligence suited the North British Railway perfectly. It justified their interest in what appeared to be a local company simply trying to improve communications for residents of the area. The West Highland Railway company was the result, and did not become part of the NBR officially until 1908.

In fact, both NBR and Caledonian rapidly made use of a 'proxy' system of promoting new extensions to their network from the 1860s onwards, when their officials and directors realised that the expense of land acquisition for a new railway could in some cases rival actual construction costs. Better to encourage local people to subscribe to a new company, create a regional air of self-help and community advancement, then hope that local landowners would offer free passage to the 'local' railway. In this way, the North British 'acquired' the Berwickshire Railway for a fraction of the cost of the Tweed Valley line farther

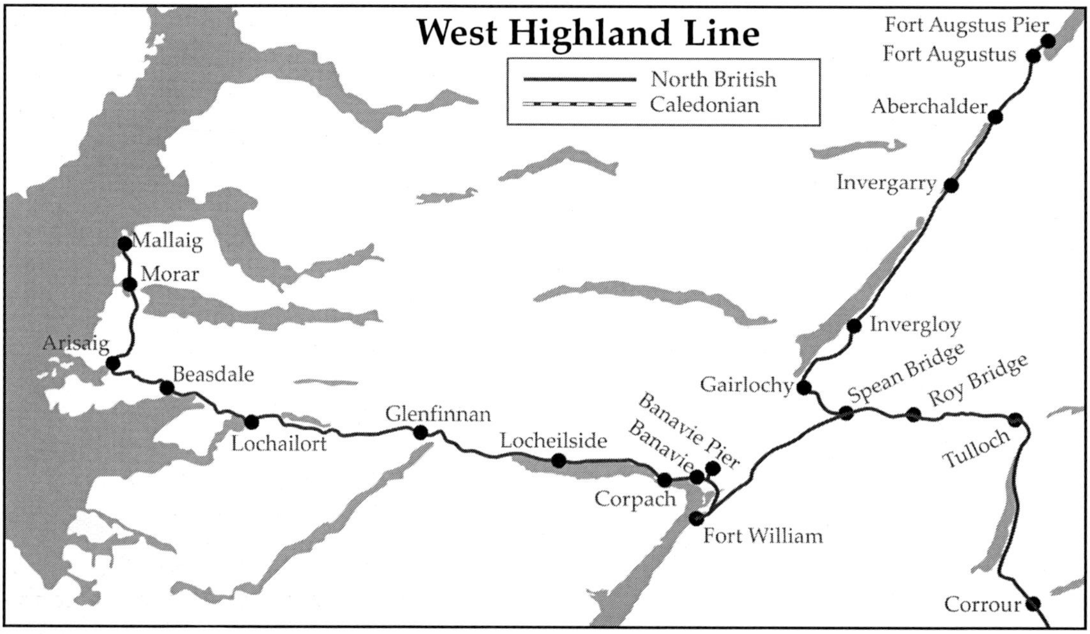

Corrour Station.

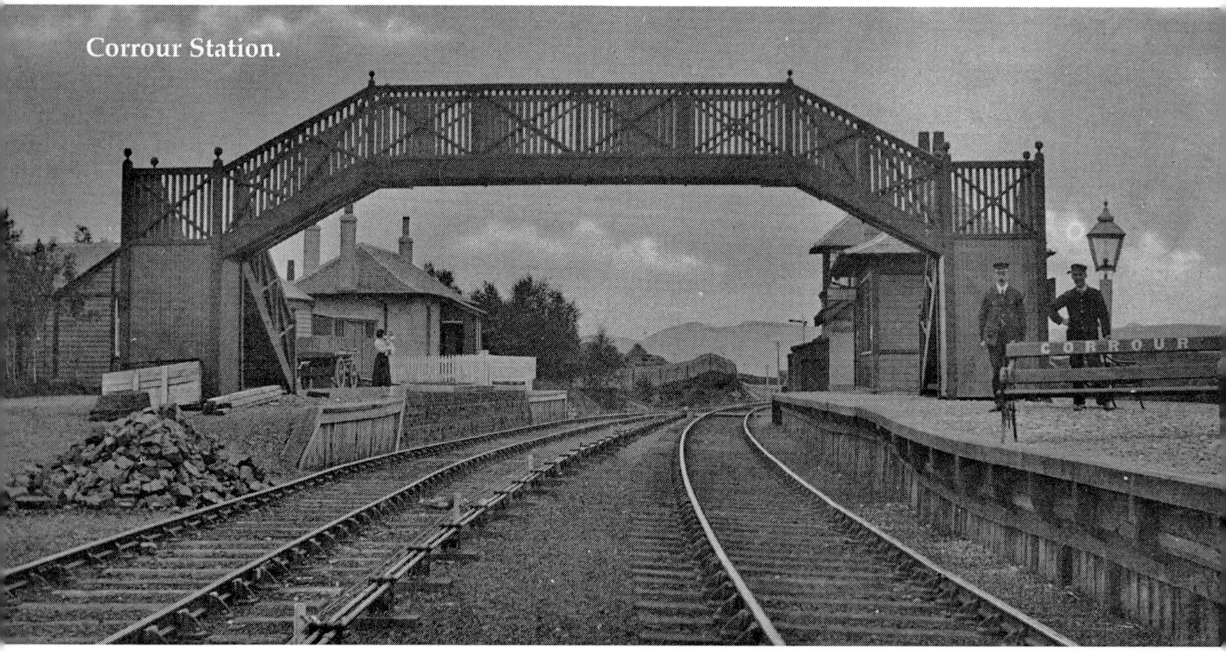

south. Peebles and Lauder were other border communities which became rail-connected in this way, and both Edinburgh and Glasgow acquired new suburban lines nominally built and owned by companies independent of the North British. The West Highland Railway was little different.

The first meeting of its board, or more correctly a steering committee at that stage, took place at Westminster on July 11th 1889. With Lord Abinger in the chair, the committee comprised Cameron of Locheil, the civil engineer Charles Forman, John Walker, General Manager of the

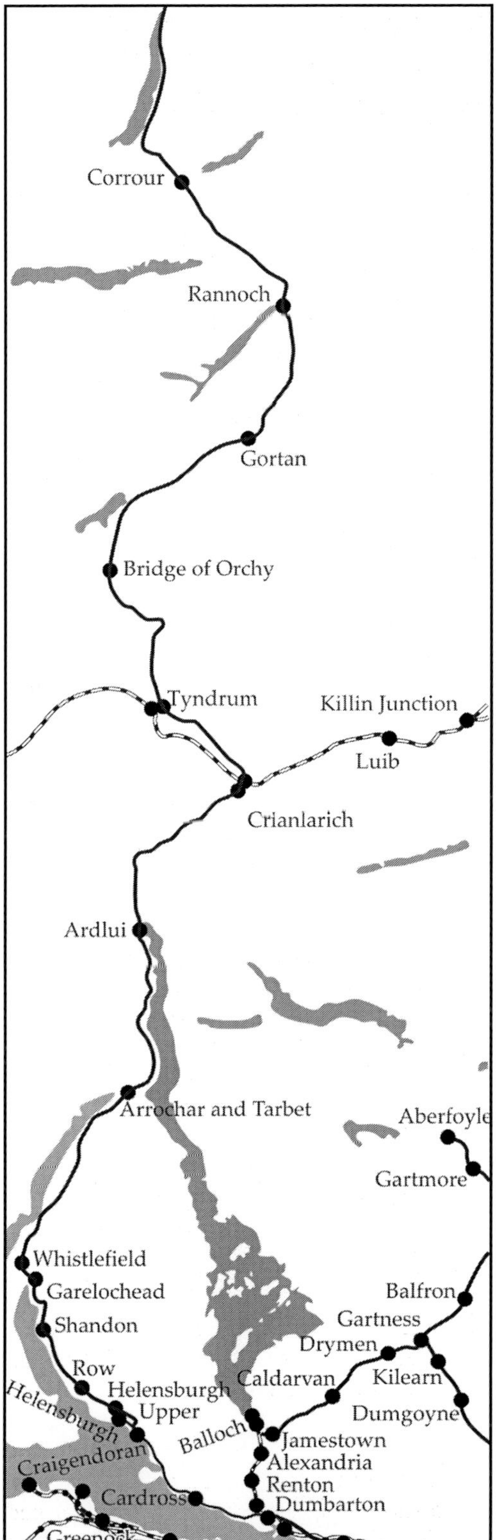

North British, and two other gentlemen. If there was any doubt of the NBR interest in this new company it would be dispelled by Walker's attendance. Not only that, but the next 'Board' meeting took place on the NBR premises in Edinburgh and George Wieland was soon appointed Company Secretary – He was of course NBR Company Secretary and held a similar, almost supervisory, position in relation to the Forth Bridge Railway.

Much of the early discussion related, naturally enough, to construction costs in the battle to penetrate this part of the Western Highlands with rails. Forman offered to oversee construction at a cost of £250 per mile, including the service of inspectors but the actual cost of building the line was estimated by prospective contractors Lucas and Aird at £508,473. A quibble immediately arose as to whether this would include the cost of laying the permanent way. However, Lord Abinger is recorded in the minutes as opining that 'the North British railway company' would be financially responsible. The words 'North British' were then scored out, and initialled. The chairman or secretary had forgotten the name of their own company! The West Highland Railway would lay its own track.

Fortunately, there is no need to describe the West Highland line in detail, as there is with the Waverley Route, since the railway to Fort William and Mallaig is still very much part of the present-day system. Any author describing it can hardly do better than refer the reader to the definitive book entitled simply *The West Highland Railway* by the late John Thomas. Author of many books on Scottish railways, this is arguably his best; in particular the legal shenanigans which went on before Fort William was reached in 1894, or Mallaig in 1901, are described with a lightness of touch which is the sign of an author in complete charge of his material.

The later Mallaig extension was effectively government-funded, much to the fury of the NBR's rivals, at a time when privatisation (usually without government handouts) was seen as the only way to capitalise major construction projects. 42 miles in length, the extension was supposed to open up a route to market for the fish produce of the western coastline and the Western Isles, although tourism became its principal function.

An unexpected development which brought the NBR to within yards of Loch Ness was the Invergarry & Fort Augustus Railway. This materialised as a result of a genuine private initiative; this was no proxy railway, like the West Highland, to which it was connected. 24 miles in length, the line was proposed in 1896 to run from Spean Bridge up the Great Glen to Fort Augustus at the south end of Loch Ness. There was even an extension on to a pier on the loch itself, effectively part of the Caledonian Canal. Despite the lack of population, and poor agricultural potential, local landowner and brewing magnate Lord Burton, believed that it could stimulate the local economy – despite the mass of evidence that, in rural areas, this was one thing that railways could not be depended on to do! Burton even determined to build three intermediate stations, while the three-quarter mile extension on to Loch Ness would have an opening bridge over the Caledonian Canal, as well as its own viaduct over the River Oich (this in addition to the viaducts planned for the Spean and Gloy). There was even a tunnel and enough land purchased to allow for double track.

Needless to say, the Highland Railway was extremely nervous about this interloper, pushing its rails to within 30 miles of Inverness. From 1903 the Highland negotiated to operate the new line, but soon discovered that revenue was negligible. Four years later it was the turn of the North British to try to make a go of the line, but it took a grant from local government – surely one of the first in Britain – to make it worth the company's while. Surprisingly in

Fort William Station with Holmes designed 4-4-0 No. 227.

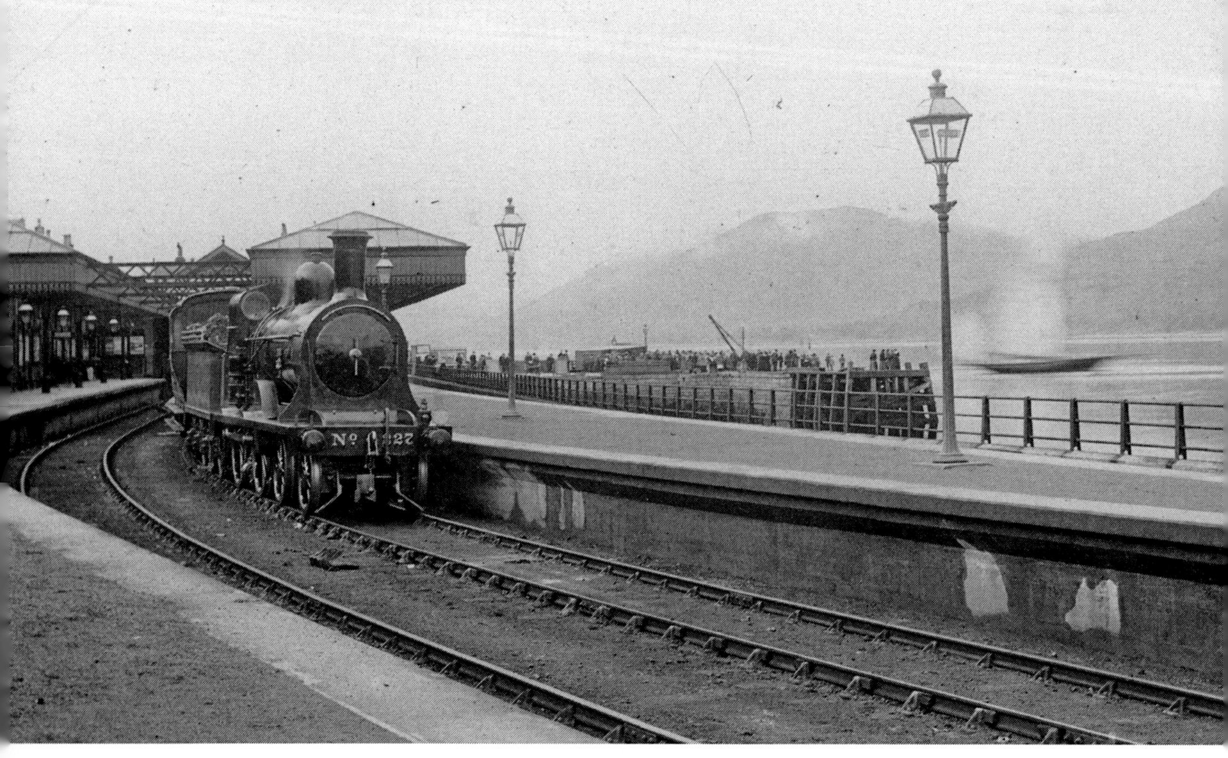

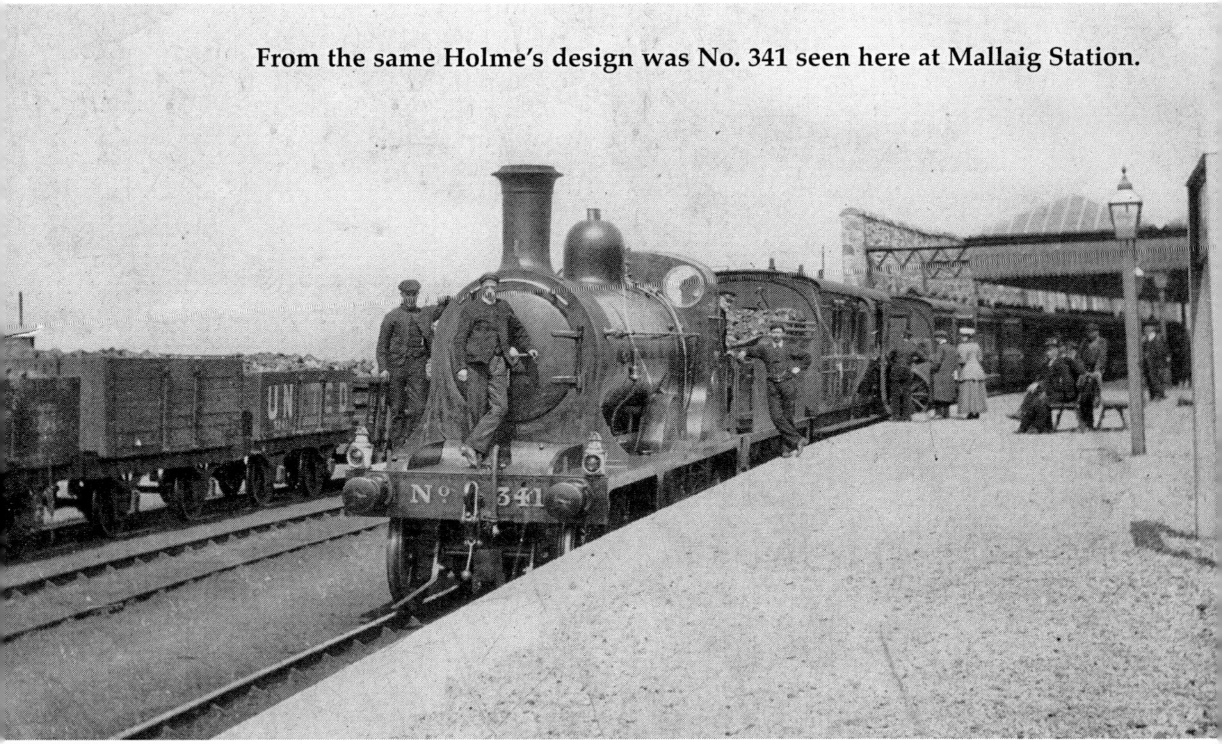

From the same Holme's design was No. 341 seen here at Mallaig Station.

the circumstances, passenger services lasted until 1933 before the inevitable withdrawal, while freight carried on until 1946. The line was however, nothing more than a fascinating footnote in the history of Highland transport.

Motive power on the West Highland line was always going to be challenged by the severe nature of the inclines. For passenger services on the line when new, Matthew Holmes designed a class of 4-4-0 with 67 inch driving wheels in 1894. These 'West Highland Bogies' did not enjoy the same high reputation as other NBR classes with the same wheel arrangement, and their Stirling-type 'cabs' – little more than a weather board – should have had the rail unions up in arms! A later class designed exclusively for the West Highland, the 'Glen' 4-4-0s, were more successful, working on the lines for more than 30 years, as well as spreading out into the rest of the system.

When the LNER took over in 1923, Gresley introduced six-coupled engines on to the line, initially ex-Great Northern K2s. He followed this up with more modern 'Mogul' types, including the excellent K4 class, while also experimenting with his lightweight *Bantam Cock* 2-6-2, a kind of go-anywhere V2. This proved a popular hard-working engine, along with its sister unofficially named 'Bantam Hen', but their construction was too expensive to perpetuate in wartime. In later years B1 and 'Black Five' 4-6-0s monopolised the line until the arrival of diesels.

Suffice to say that the North British Railway added a major extension to its system by supporting and, in December 1908, taking over, the West Highland Railway. The line was never profitable, but the NBR, rightly or wrongly, saw an unspecified approach to Inverness from the south-west direction as a possible bonus, while its handling of government negotiations to extend the WHR to Mallaig represented good business practice.

Accidents

The Tay Bridge disaster of 1879, with its toll of 75 needless deaths, was the worst moment in the history of the North British Railway. There were however a number of other accidents which should be considered, even although it is fair to say that the NBR was not one of the nation's more reckless carriers.

The next worst accident, in number of casualties, took place on the jointly-owned tracks of the Dundee & Arbroath Railway in 1906, the NBR being one of the joint owners. In atrocious conditions on a late December evening, an NBR express, working on an interval system in absence of reliable signalling, ran into the back of an earlier train stuck in snow at Elliot Junction. Even although the impact speed was only 20 mph, no fewer than 22 passengers and railwaymen died.

Driver Gourlay, in charge of the express, was tried for manslaughter, and evidence was presented suggesting that he had been drunk. This was impossible to prove as a well-meaning official had given him brandy immediately after the accident, despite the fact that he was obviously suffering from shock. Despite this, and despite the Dundee & Arbroath's failure to send out fogmen on a night of poor visibility, Driver Gourlay was sentenced to five months imprisonment, later reduced to three.

Most of the NBR's accidents happened, perhaps not surprisingly, on the intensively busy Edinburgh-Glasgow line; indeed, there had been two particularly bad incidents before the NBR took control of this line in 1865. In later NBR years, 16 passengers were killed in a crash at Manuel in 1874, which could have been prevented if there had been interlocking between points and signals, and two accidents happened at Ratho, in 1914 and again in 1917. There

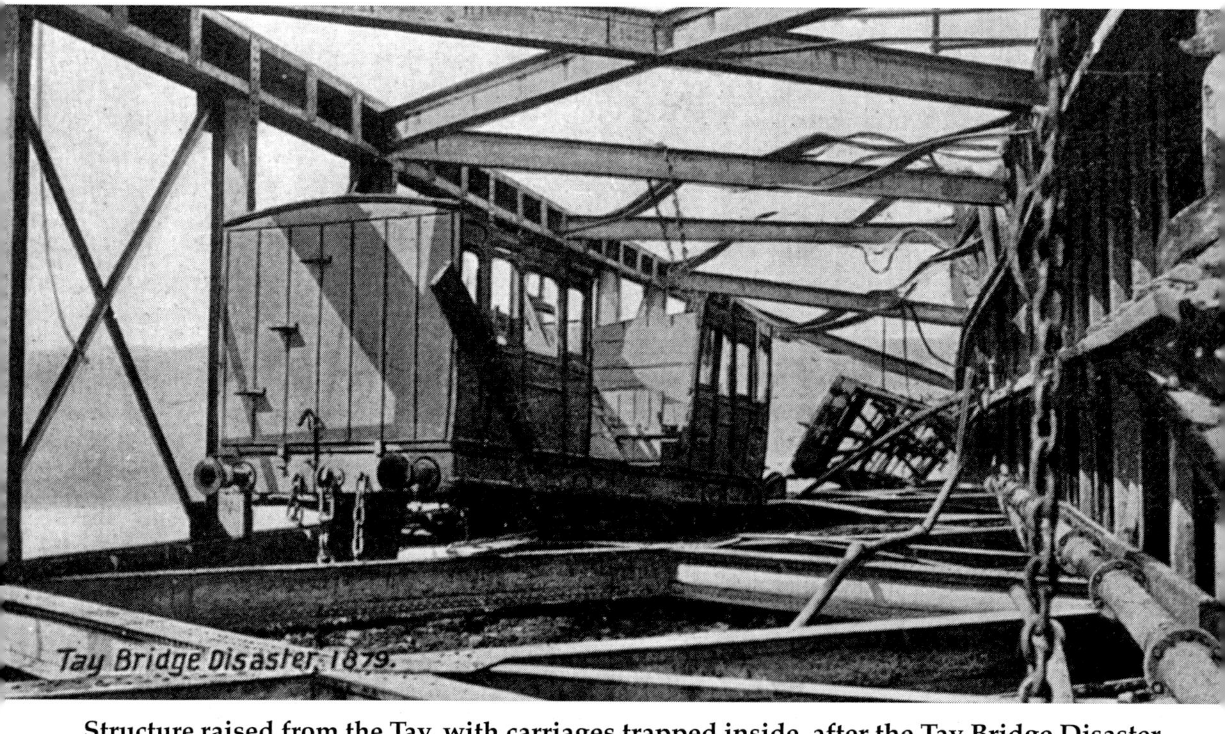

Structure raised from the Tay, with carriages trapped inside, after the Tay Bridge Disaster.

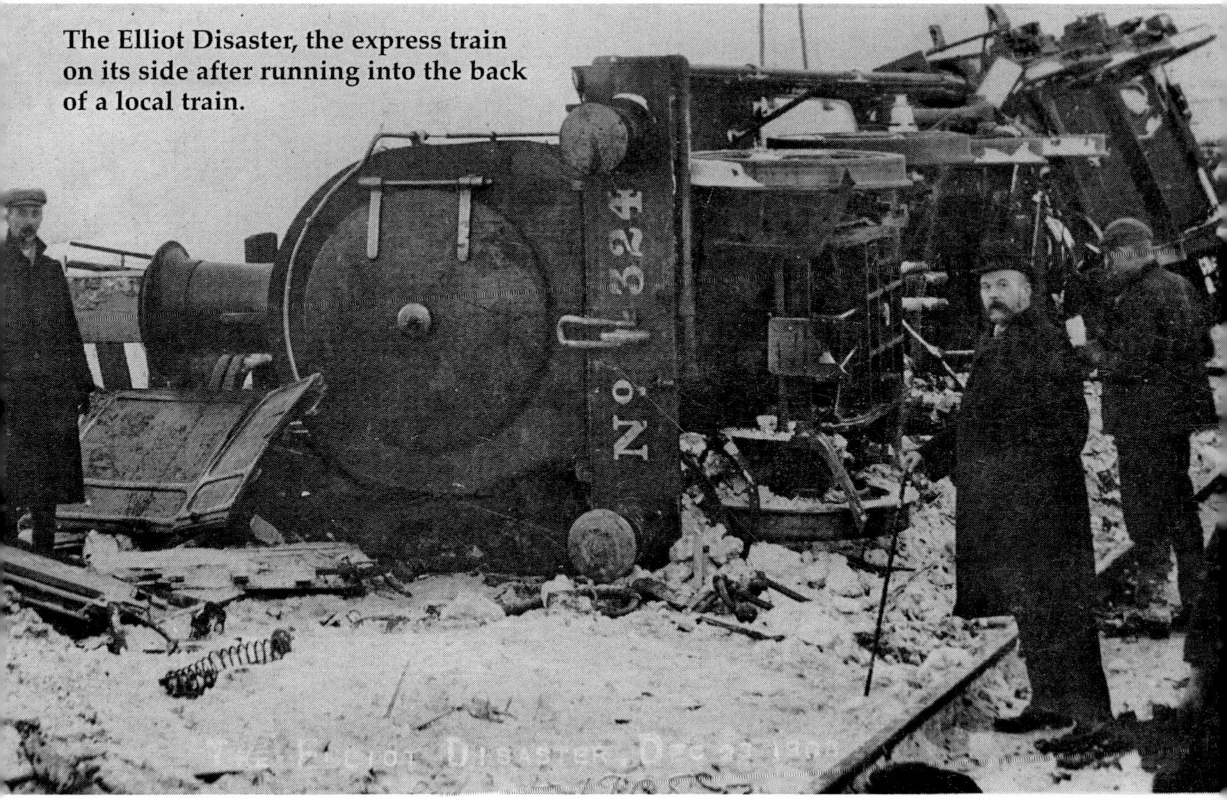
The Elliot Disaster, the express train on its side after running into the back of a local train.

were no fatalities in the first of these two, but 12 people were killed, and 44 injured, in the second. On the latter occasion there was a collision between 'Scott' 4-4-0 No. 421 *Jingling Geordie* and 'Atlantic' No. 874 *Dunedin,* caused by irregular working practices at the junction of the line from Kirkliston and South Queensferry.

As pointed out by this author in his book on the Caledonian Railway – which suffered Britain's worst-ever accident at Quintinshill in 1915 – it didn't seem to occur to the railway authorities to install track-circuiting at important stations and junctions, if not throughout their entire systems. Yet when something went wrong, it was the staff who were blamed.

No less than 43 years earlier, track-circuiting was first tried out successfully in the USA. It was experimented with at King's Cross terminus in London, but not applied nationwide. It is difficult to see why not.

All that was required was a small electrical charge, usually no more than 100 volts, to be fed along the rail itself, within signalling sections. Any train entering the section automatically short-circuited the current, illuminating a control panel light in the nearby box. It was a simple concept, cheap to run, and above all, was 'fail safe', with any breakdown in the system indicating a broken circuit and therefore an occupied section, either automatically setting signals at danger, or at least giving an emergency signal to the signalman.

However, one accident on the NBR which track-circuiting could not have prevented, took place at Dunbar on the night of September 1st 1882. There was a tremendous explosion on the locomotive working a Leith-Berwick goods train, the driver being killed outright.

A Board of Trade enquiry was held, but no cause could be established. It was not unknown for enginemen to disable safety valves to avoid wasting excess steam; an action whose stupidity is beyond comment. This does not seem to have been the case here – it would have been technically near-impossible. However, the Inspector was very suspicious when it was established that a wine and spirits merchant was travelling (unauthorised) in the cab of the engine, but quite what the significance of this was, neither he nor anyone else could determine.

The Board of Trade inspector concluded that the boiler had exploded because it was subjected to sudden increased steam pressure. As historian Hamilton Ellis wrote, it was 'about as helpful a statement [as saying] that a ship had suddenly sunk because a large hole had appeared below the waterline'!

The safety record of the North British was not exemplary, but was considerably better than might have been expected of a line which suffered a fatality on its very first day.

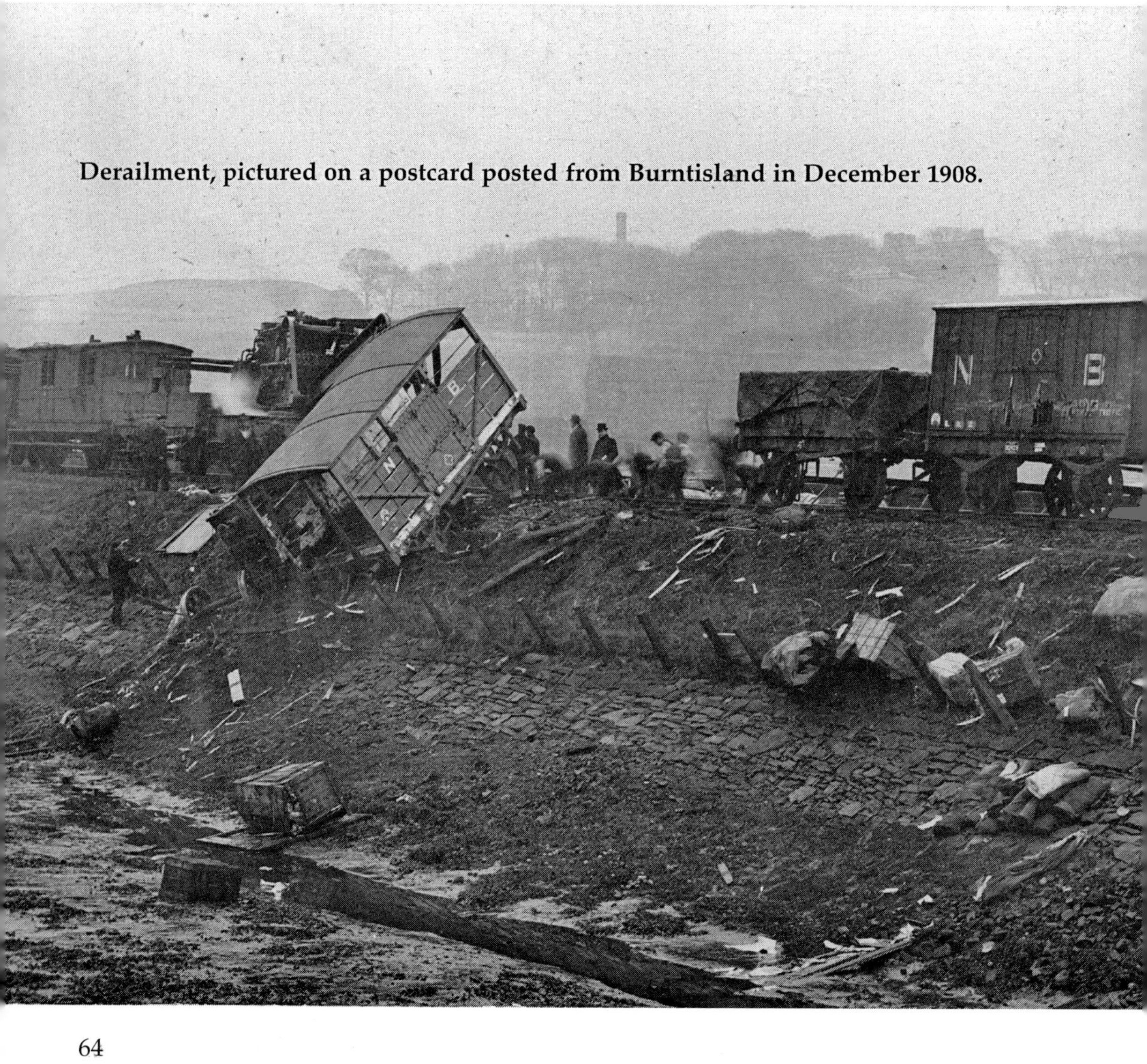

Derailment, pictured on a postcard posted from Burntisland in December 1908.

Racing Days

With so much duplication built into the 19th century British railway network, it's perhaps surprising that there were not more examples of racing between companies serving the same destination. Surprising or not, history shows us that, with the exception of some competition among English companies to bring trans-Atlantic passengers and mails from southern ports up to London, Britain's only race-tracks were the East and West Coast lines, between London, Edinburgh, and Aberdeen.

Racing took place in three separate summer seasons – 1888, 1895, and 1901. The first of these passages of competition did not involve the North British – despite the fact that its premier main line, between Berwick-on-Tweed and Edinburgh, represented the 'final straight' for the East Coast racer. A brief explanation is necessary for this, as it relates to a problem that was one of the causes of the 1901 race as well.

We have already seen that the NB pushed south from Hawick on a route which would allow a secondary route into the north of England via Riccarton and Hexham. When complete in 1862, this, the Border Counties Railway, inspired the NB Board to accept an offer of running-powers into Newcastle over North Eastern Railway metals in return for dropping opposition to a NER takeover of this very route, hitherto the Newcastle and Carlisle Railway.

Also, so desperate was the Edinburgh company to gain its own foothold in Newcastle, that it agreed to NER running-powers all the way from Berwick and into Edinburgh – and even beyond.

This extraordinary agreement was entered into by the North British on the basis of a completely inflated opinion of the viability of the Border Counties line, one which the NER clearly did not share, and rightly so. Historian E.L. Ahrons decreed that the North British had 'sold its birthright for a mess of pottage'.

For decades to come, the sight of NBR engines trundling branch line trains into Newcastle Central was always something of a curiosity, while NER engines and enginemen took up permanent quarters at firstly, St. Margaret's Depot, and latterly, Haymarket, ostentatiously outclassing the 'top link' crews working at these sheds. When the first Gresley Pacifics were allocated to Haymarket in 1924, they were mainly crewed by ex-NER men, with Scottish crews hurriedly having to learn the road south of Berwick.

From 1869, no express train for the south headed out of Waverley behind one of the NB's own engines until the Settle-Carlisle line was opened in 1876. Scotland's own railway historian, John Thomas, believed that the new supremacy of the NER worked in favour of the travelling public, not least by omitting the need for engine-changing at Berwick. However, this could have been facilitated by simply sharing Edinburgh-Newcastle through workings between NBR and NER on a running-powers ratio which would have reflected the respective track mileages (in other words, say, four through trains headed by NER engines, as against three by NBR). Running powers could then have been offered the NER on the Border Counties line, at least as far as Hawick, since at Hexham the NER had the nearest large operating centre.

Instead, the NBR directors so regretted their 1862 agreement that they contested it in front of no fewer than eleven tribunals and in two visits to the House of Lords. Throughout all this time, the North Eastern showed itself to be an intransigent and insensitive negotiator,

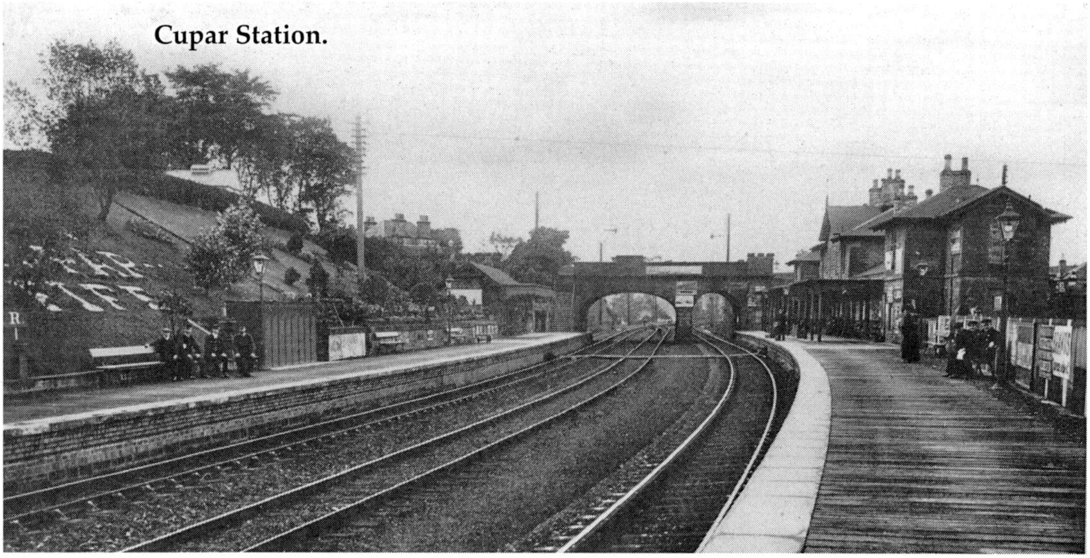

Cupar Station.

although it could reasonably argue that the public seemed perfectly happy with the arrangement it had so triumphantly concluded.

This explains why the North British was a mere spectator as the timetables were ripped up in July and August 1888, and all four competing companies, the London & North Western and Caledonian railway companies on the west, and Great Northern and North Eastern on the east, brought London-Edinburgh times down to $6\frac{1}{2}$ hours. But when a second passage of racing flared again in 1895, the destination was Aberdeen, and this meant that the North British was going to be very much involved.

With the North Eastern bringing the overnight 8pm ex-King's Cross into Waverley, it was up to the newcomer to take it forward via the Bridges route to Aberdeen. While the East Coast companies now had a shorter mileage – King's Cross to Kinnaber Junction (where the NB and CR lines merged) was 485 miles as compared to 502 miles from Euston – this advantage was illusory.

Only the Waverley Route could compare with the Edinburgh-Aberdeen main line for sharp curves, steep inclines, and speed restrictions. Up until 1960 no train was timetabled to travel between Edinburgh and Dundee in less than 81 minutes for the 59 taxing miles between these cities, while north of Dundee, part of the route was actually single-line, with speed having to be reduced to allow the crews to exchange tablets (giving permission for occupying the section, something more akin to branch line working). In contrast the Caledonian had a beautifully laid out main line through Strathmore, guaranteeing a fast approach to Kinnaber. And the Caledonian, speed-hardened and noted performers in the 1888 contest, had no intention of being beaten by their traditional rivals!

Readers wishing to learn more about this extraordinary sequence of competitive railroading, can do no better than read O.S. Nock's *Railway Race to the North* (unfortunately out of print at the time of writing, although well worth searching for second-hand). Mr Nock is careful not to name the winner of the 1895 contest, but it has to be the West Coast consortium, if only for their determination to race night after night until their rivals cried 'Enough'. Which is exactly what the East Coast did after their overnight run on August 21st and 22nd, a journey which ended in an impressive victory, with a North British Holmes 4-4-0 crossing the 'finishing line' first.

Suffice to say that the North British, newcomers to racing though their crews were, made a contribution which was absolutely unique. While light filled the eastern sky on the morning of August 22nd, Holmes 4-4-0 No. 293 reeled off the 59 miles between Waverley and Dundee in exactly 'even time' – 59 minutes start-to-stop. From here, after a change of engine in a mere two minutes, sister engine No. 262 took the racer forward through Kinnaber, with no 'Caley' train in sight, reaching Aberdeen in 77 minutes for the 71 miles on the most northern part of the run. Mr Nock professed himself unable to identify the crews responsible, but the RCTS history of the class of 4-4-0s (both of the '633' class), credited drivers J. McGregor and C. Spalding, and firemen J. Berry and J. Anton, as the men responsible for the Edinburgh-Dundee and Dundee-Aberdeen records respectively.

What was unique about these performances was that they were never to be equalled in the next 80 years! While the spectacular work done by all the other racing companies would eventually be overtaken by trains headed by steam engines of greater power in decades to come, this never happened on the Edinburgh-Aberdeen route. Indeed, when diesel services were first introduced in 1959, the timing between the cities was 3 hours (something Reid's Atlantics could achieve in Edwardian times). Yet the 1895 racer did the journey 41 minutes faster!

Nor was this timing a fluke. Two nights previously, the Edinburgh-Dundee stretch was accomplished in 64 minutes, still far better than anything scheduled for Pacific power in later years, while on the morning of 21st August 1895, the 4-4-0 concerned reached the Tayside city in 30 seconds over the even hour, not much more than a minute slower than the record run of the following evening.

Yet this was the only occasion when the East Coast could claim supremacy during the later stages of the race, proving that its outcome was decided, not on the swaying footplates of steam engines pounding through the night, but on the surveyor's drawing-board. The Caledonian enjoyed by far a better line to run on, in terms of easy curvature and reasonable gradients, and the NB was never going to find it easy to better that. The latter's main line to Aberdeen, like so many of its routes, was built piece-meal and engineered as economically as possible.

This was to be demonstrated to even greater effect on the Waverley Route, when an intriguing coda to the 1888 and 1895 races emerged in 1901. On this occasion, the NBR was asked by its Midland partner to improve Anglo-Scottish journey times, and found itself guaranteeing its southern partner to take the 9.30 am St.Pancras-Edinburgh over the Waverley Route from Carlisle in 135 minutes. This was five minutes faster than the previous best time, with no stops for water.

Meanwhile, the North Eastern, the NBR's supposed ally on the East Coast, decided to accelerate the northbound 'Flying Scotsman' by 15 minutes to ensure that it was not blocked by any late running of the St. Pancras service at Portobello East junction, $3^1/_2$ miles east of Waverley. The NERs acceleration was a breach of the 1896 agreement already signed by the companies operating over the Border, intended to assuage public concern about racing following the Preston accident in that year (not actually involving a racing train, but one where there had been excessive speed on curving track).

The North Eastern however, believed that neither the Midland nor the North British would be able to keep to their accelerated schedule, and brought their timing forward to reduce delays to their own train. This inevitably led to the prospect of Portobello East becoming a new 'Kinnaber'. While the companies tried to play down the concept of racing, a number of newspapers, not least the populist *Daily Mail*, 'wrote up' what it saw as a conflict, beginning on July 1st 1901.

Headed by Holmes 4-4-0 No. 738, the St. Pancras traversed the Waverley Route in 126 minutes – a record for a service train on this most difficult of lines. Despite this, it still played second fiddle to the NER whose locomotive No 2015 came up from Newcastle in 140 minutes. O.S. Nock dismisses this timing as 'not anything very wonderful', yet there is evidence that NBR signalmen north of Berwick delayed the NER competitor by some seven minutes (it was, after all, running well ahead of booked time).

Mr Nock in fact seems to have lost interest in the contest at around this point, being apparently unaware of what happened on July 5th, the Thursday of that week. With the newspapers reporting *all* arrival times at Edinburgh, and indicating that the NER appeared unbeatable, the LNWR and Caledonian could stand it no more. On the 5th, the 10 am out of Euston was run as two sections north of Crewe, and when the 'Caley' took over ahead of schedule at Carlisle, their crew didn't even wait for the timetabled departure time. Off they went, with a Dunalastair III achieving a remarkable time of 108 minutes to Edinburgh, inclusive of two signal delays at Beattock. Arrival at Princes Street Station was no less than 35 minutes ahead of time, much to the astonishment of the porters.

Of course, this simply meant that the North British was now third into Edinburgh, instead of second, but, with the Caledonian winning again on the Friday, a major effort was made on the following Monday. The Midland was no doubt being urged to improve its delivery at Carlisle (after all, this acceleration was all their idea!) and it appears that one of the new '2606' 4-4-0s was drafted into service north of Leeds. For once the Midland train came in early, by five minutes, so the NB did not have to repeat its frantic running of the previous week, when a total of no less than 24 minutes had been saved north of Carlisle to recover time lost south of there by the English company. A 135 minute run to Edinburgh resulted, and cheering crowds greeted the North British arrival ahead of the North Eastern. The 'Caley' came in early at the other end of Princes Street, but was still two minutes behind the NB engine's time.

Analysis of the respective NBR/NER times (see this author's *The Railway Race to Scotland 1901*) suggests that, in fact, the North Eastern express was actually first to Portobello East, or at least to Joppa, immediately to the east, with the NBR signalman accepting the St. Pancras train first as soon as it reached the box south of him, at Niddrie. Nor was this unsporting – the NER was not running to its own published timetable, nor was it abiding by the 1896 minimum-time agreement governing Anglo-Scottish services. Yet this company was supposed to be an ally! Once again the deadly legacy of the 1862 agreement made itself felt.

The NB was in an anomalous position in having to deal equally with two opposing factions. On one occasion, the Midland dispatched an employee to Waverley to count the posters advertising East Coast travel! So it is no surprise that the 1901 race was allowed to fade away, particularly with the company having to handle so much excursion traffic at a time of Scottish holidays. On the Saturday of that week, no fewer than 2,000 extra travellers boarded trains at Waverley for Kirkcaldy, and 500 more required transport to the now-vanished station at Dalkeith.

In the long term, the three races of 1888, 1895, and 1901 had a disastrous effect on Anglo-Scottish express services. The 1896 agreement, with its upper limit of $8^1/_4$ hours between London and Edinburgh and Glasgow, was made to reassure any public concerns about safety, but became more binding as the years went on, resulting in the LNER being constrained to operate its new Gresley Pacifics, and the LMS its 'Royal Scot' locomotives, to the same timings that 4-4-0 locomotives had attained with ease in the 1890s!

This was nothing less than a cartel against the public interest, although the media, less analytical than nowadays, failed to question why no accelerations seemed possible on such trains as the 'Flying Scotsman'. Not surprisingly, rival modes of transport started up, particularly bus services, although in 1928 it was noticeable that the operators could not guarantee any time of arrival.

The NBR and its successor, the LNER, couldn't even kill off the coastal passenger services between Edinburgh and London. As late as the 1930s, travellers were still taking sea voyages between these cities! And all because the rail companies imperiously believed that the public would accept their 'take it or leave it' attitude of imposing lax timetabling and fares far higher than those offered by the rivals old and new.

Although there were rail accelerations from 1932, a direct result of this snail's pace of transport on the railways came not just from road and sea, but also from above. When Anglo-Scottish air services began in 1934, eight of the first 70 flights failed to reach their destination. This is not as alarming as it might sound; weather conditions forced their curtailment at an airport *en route*. But this premature introduction of air services proves that the railways' monopolistic attitude encouraged other forms of transport, even when these were not technically advanced enough to offer a reliable service.

In the light of all this, the LNER and LMS insistence on continuing the 1896 agreement up to 1932 – deliberately keeping Anglo-Scottish expresses down to a 48 mph average speed – was commercial madness. Even racing made more sense than that.

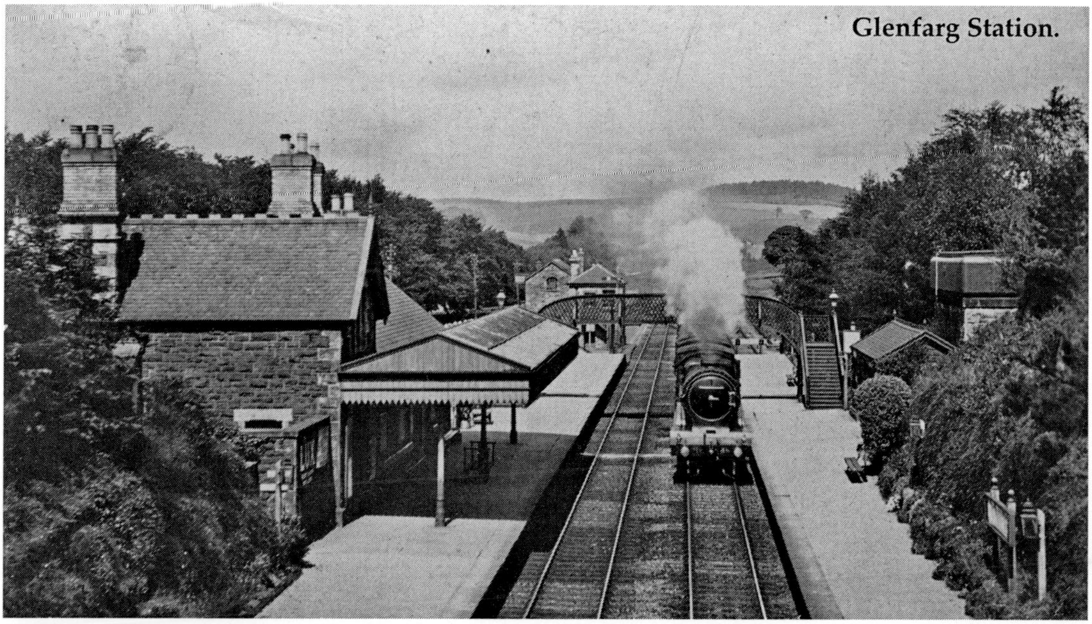

Glenfarg Station.

Steamers

Operating ships did not present Scottish rail companies with any kind of new challenge. From the first decade of passenger-carrying operations on Scotland's main lines, the railway companies were having to come to terms with the demands of topography, particularly the need to cross rivers and estuaries by ferry-boat.

The North British Railway was particularly affected by geographical problems of this kind, especially after its takeover of the Edinburgh Perth and Dundee company, which operated ferry services across both Forth and Tay. In the same decade, the absorption of the Edinburgh & Glasgow line meant that the Union Canal came under NBR ownership. In contrast, the Caledonian, conceived as a kind of 'Grand Junction' line, was more internalised and less immediately involved in ferry crossing as an integral part of its network.

In 1862, at the same time as coming to grips with the everyday business of crossing the Forth and Tay by boat, the NBR committed itself to maritime operations on the Solway. This was done 'from scratch' as it were, with the purchase of the paddle-steamer *Ariel* for no less than £8,500, to operate out of the company's new Solway port of Silloth, reached by branch line from Carlisle. When some shareholders expressed unease at the railway company becoming directly involved in ship-owning, the NBR bowed to this reasonable sentiment, and the nominally-separate North British Steam Packet Company was set up soon afterwards.

Working out of its new port of Silloth in Cumberland, the NBR found the Silloth-Liverpool run to be highly remunerative as no tolls had to be paid on freight from anywhere in the NBR system traversing the Carlisle rail network, since the Canal Junction area was not owned by the Caledonian. For a time, Dublin and Belfast also saw NBR colours regularly, but neither route could produce the same turnover as the Liverpool run.

Marmion.

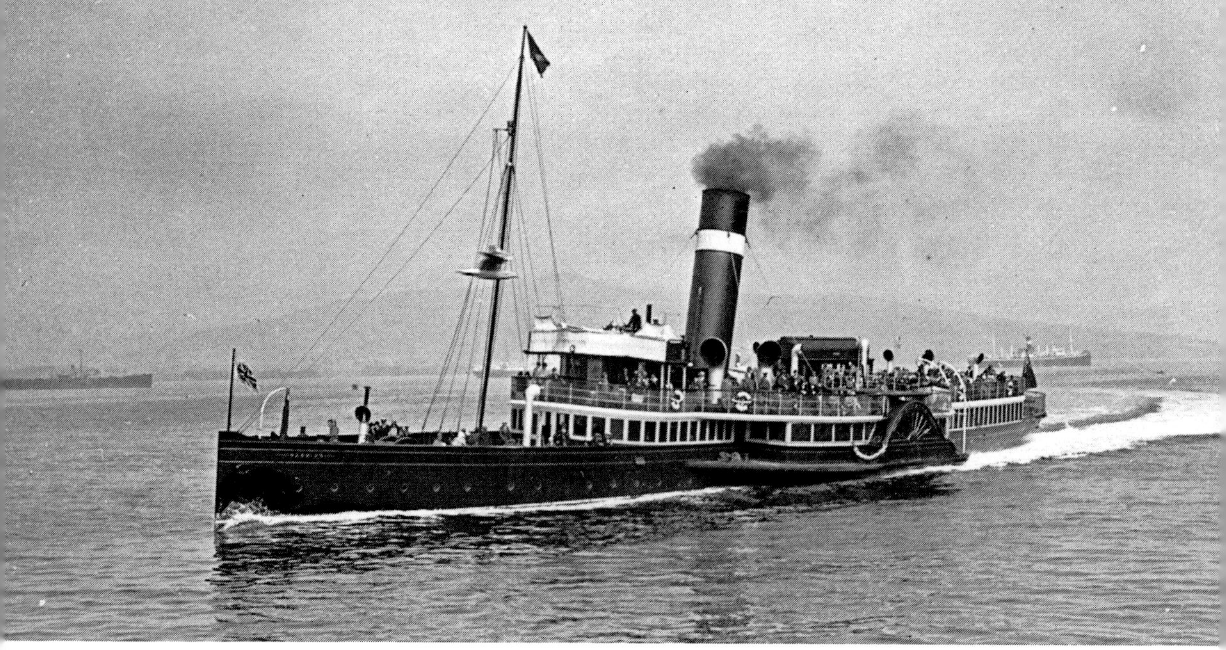

The expertise built up by the NBR in this aspect of transport proved useful when the company began to consolidate its influence on the west coast, particularly the north bank of the Clyde. The sponsoring of the Glasgow City and District line under the city and then westwards, gave the NBR the opportunity to participate in the steamer traffic which already occupied the Caledonian and Glasgow & South Western railways in deadly rivalry.

Centering on the Clyde, steamers fulfilled two functions – one was purely recreational, taking Glasgow holidaymakers 'doon the watter' – but there was a more workaday function required in providing ferry services to Arran, the Kyles of Bute, Ireland, even the Isle of Man. By the beginning of the 20th century, no less than two-thirds of all the vessels plying the Clyde or Loch Lomond were railway-owned.

Unfortunately, the NBR got off to an unhappy start in this area, its choice of Helensburgh proving to be unsuitable as a base, and early operations to the Kyles lasted barely a single season in 1866. Thereafter, Craigendoran, a mile to the east of Helensburgh, was chosen as a cruising base, and the NBR committed itself fully to maritime activities on the Clyde from the completion of the pier facilities at Craigendoran from 1883.

Eight vessels were registered by the NBSP for passenger-carrying between 1888 and the First World War. Historian John Thomas described these as 'the least flamboyant of the railway-owned ships on the Clyde' (rather like NBR trains!), although he conceded that the *Marmion* of 1906 was one of the fastest ships to be found on the Firth. As might be gathered from the foregoing ship's name, the North British Steam Packet Company – to give the NBR its full name in its aquatic guise – had the happy habit of naming its vessels after Sir Walter's Scott's novels.

Not only was she fast, but *Marmion* distinguished herself in military service. Converted to minesweeping duties in both First and Second World Wars, this NBR steamer survived three successful trips to Dunkirk in 1940 to help rescue the battered British Expeditionary Force. Unfortunately she was sunk by German aircraft during an attack on Harwich in the following year and although raised, had to be broken up. Another NBR vessel which saw naval service was the *Talisman*, being present at the D-Day landings and the first Allied ship to enter Antwerp Harbour after the German retreat. She emerged unscathed from the conflict, but the 1899-built *Waverley* failed to survive the Second World War as it had the First, being bombed and sunk at Dunkirk in 1940.

In addition to the Clyde itself, North British colours (featuring funnels with red, white, and black bands in ascending order) were also seen on Loch Lomond, the Dumbarton and Balloch Joint Line Committee being jointly operated by the NBR and the Caledonian, with four paddle-steamers on the loch from 1883. These provided a year-long service, with many of the lochside communities having no rail or road access at that time.

Unfortunately, this aspect of NBR operations has not lasted to the present day. Craigendoran lost its maritime services in 1972, while the *Maid of the Loch*, the beneficiary of the NBR and LNER pleasure-ship tradition on Loch Lomond, has, at the time of writing, been tied up by the pier at Balloch for many years. Although, the ship is now actively being restored with the intention of having it return to cruising in 2018. In contrast, the *Waverley*, a postwar vessel built by the LNER, still operates as the last sea-going paddle-steamer in the world, a proud memento of a once-prosperous maritime operation.

So, although it may be its Clyde steamers for which the NB's maritime arm is remembered, it was in fact on the Forth, Tay, and Solway that the company had first taken to the water.

Hotels

As a company which had grown rich on the movement of coal, it's hardly surprising that the North British did not operate, or even aspire to own, a chain of hotels linked to its stations. In practice, the NB only entered such important cities as Aberdeen, Perth, and Carlisle, by running powers, so it is no surprise that no NBR hotels were established there (although the company had a one-third share in the Station Hotel, Perth).

Edinburgh and Glasgow did however, have their 'NB' hotels – as they were known to the inhabitants of both these cities. The Glasgow 'NB' was situated in George Square, inherited from the Edinburgh & Glasgow, but the NBR had extensively refurbished it during Edwardian times, not hesitating to give it the telegraph address of 'Attractive, Glasgow' on its reopening in 1905. But it had its shortcomings, the 84 bedrooms not enjoying hot and cold water as late as 1933, and lacking 'metropolitan sophistication', according to Glasgow station historians, Johnston and Hume. After being refurbished again in the 1970s, the hotel was sold off in 1984 for an astonishingly low sum. But the pride of the line was undoubtedly the NB Hotel in Edinburgh.

Equalled in size by the Caledonian's hotels at Glasgow Central and at the other end of Princes Street, nevertheless the Edinburgh establishment somehow drew great authority from its location, at the corner of Princes Street and North Bridge. This site had proved to be a problem during construction, as foundations had to be sunk into volcanic rock, the company soon having to pay out compensation for damaging neighbouring buildings when using dynamite. Not surprisingly, with the foundations being dug by hand, the hotel took four years to build from 1898, to the design of William Hamilton Beattie, and although described recently by one architectural author as 'lacking landmark quality', the clock tower is undeniably one of the most famous features of the Edinburgh skyline. It is now in private hands, renamed the Balmoral, but the Edinburgh tradition of the 'NB' clock being kept two minutes fast, still appears to be observed.

In retrospect, it is a little surprising that the North British did not speculate by building, or buying, hotels in such golfing centres as St. Andrews, North Berwick, and Gullane. The last-named in particular could have done with more investment of this kind – and the Gullane branch with more revenue - and one cannot help surmising that the Caledonian, which began construction of a high-class establishment at Gleneagles just before the Grouping, would not have hesitated to enter the hotel industry at these other famous golfing sites! Ironically, the company which ultimately controlled the NB's, and all other railway-owned establishments, British Transport Hotels, built the Old Course Hotel at St. Andrews in 1969. By this time, of course, the railway to St. Andrews was firmly closed.

Curiously, the North British owned at least six inns. It's not too surprising to see that these were located in Edinburgh, Glasgow, Burntisland, Dalkeith (immediately next to the station site), and Linlithgow, but the existence of a NBR-owned hostelry in Fort Augustus is more of a surprise. The company only operated the Invergarry & Fort Augustus Railway on a contractual basis, and with no great enthusiasm, given the poor financial return. The Lovat Arms was indeed a frontier-type saloon as far as the North British was concerned.

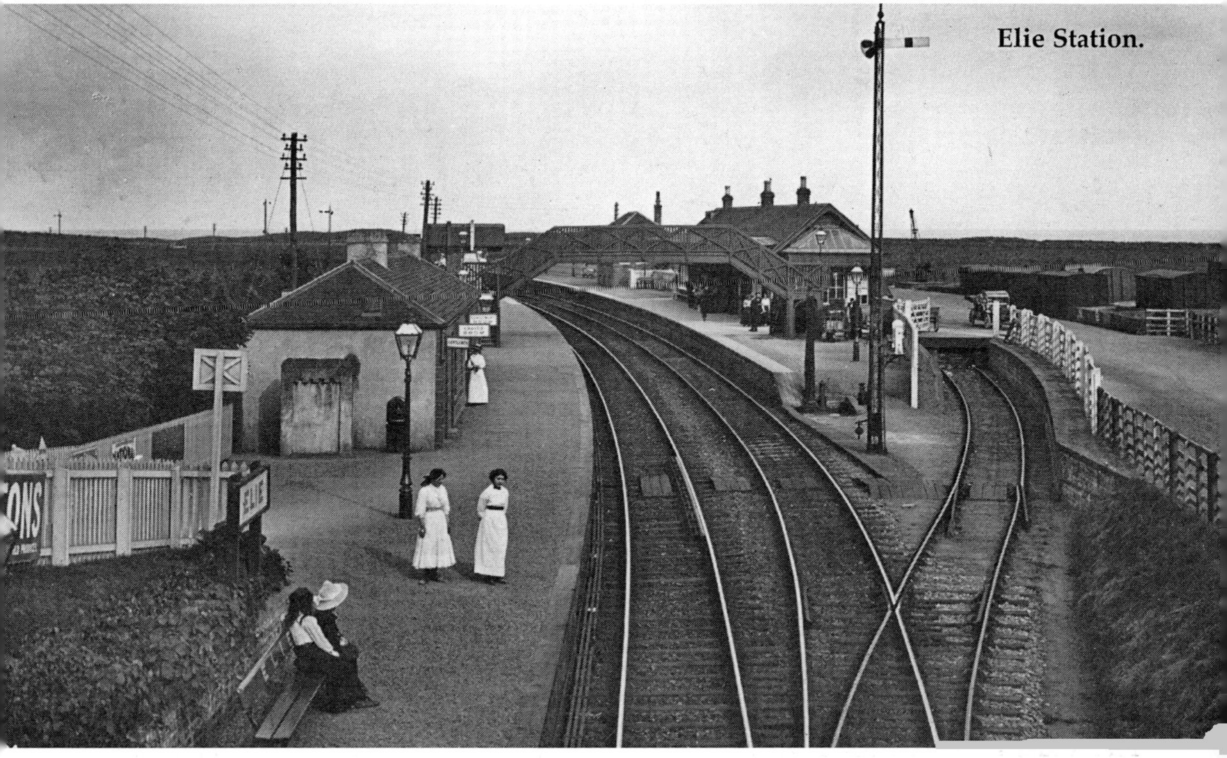

Elie Station.

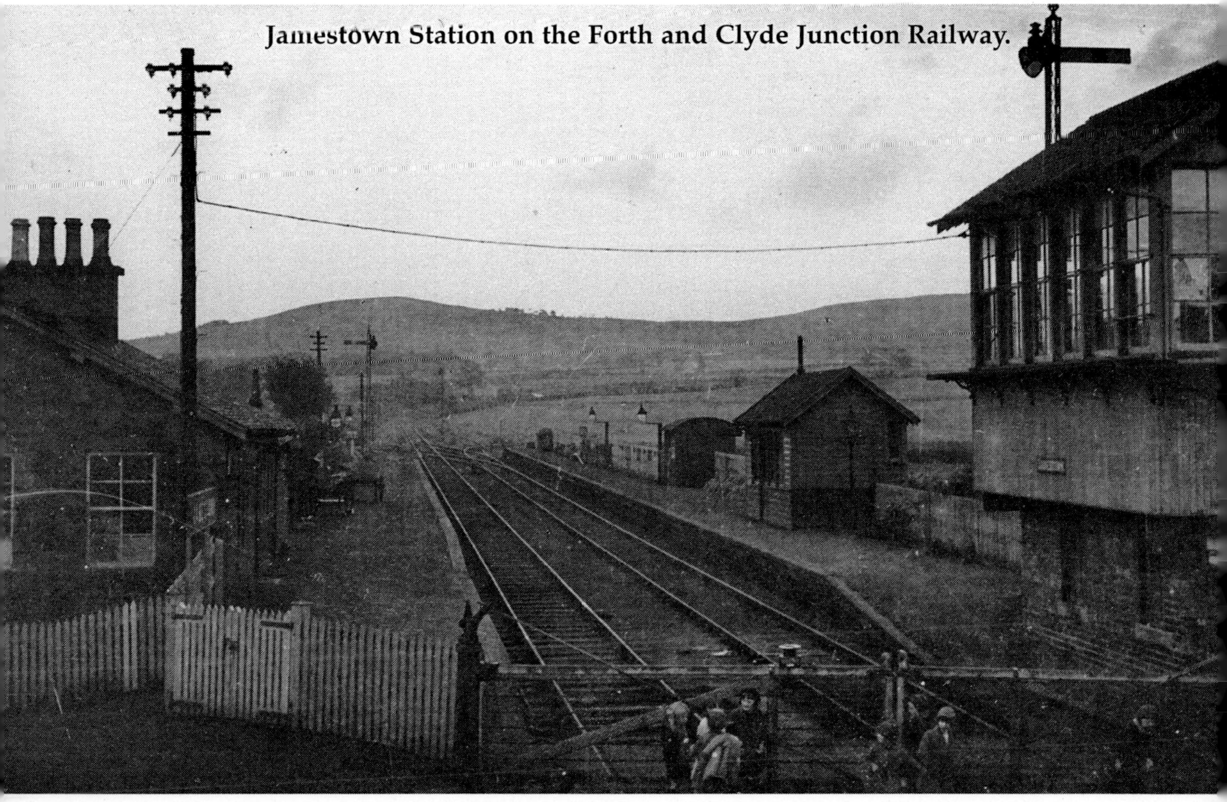

Jamestown Station on the Forth and Clyde Junction Railway.

A PUBLIC MEETING

OF THE

INHABITANTS

OF THE DISTRICTS OF

DUNOON, KIRN, & HUNTER'S QUAY,

WILL BE HELD IN THE

BURGH HALL,

ON FRIDAY FIRST, 13th APRIL,

For the purpose of considering the propriety of Memorialising the Directors of the North British Railway Company to continue their efforts to obtain the sanction of Parliament this Session to their Bill for an Extension of the Railway to Helensburgh Pier, or its revival under more favourable circumstances in a future Parliamentary Session.

PROVOST MELVILLE IN THE CHAIR.

ADDRESSES will be given by Various Gentlemen.

Chair to be taken at EIGHT o'Clock.

The Proposed Extension of the Helensburgh Railway would be of great advantage to the Inhabitants of Dunoon, Kirn, and Hunter's Quay.

DUNOON, 11TH APRIL, 1877. PRINTED AT THE "DUNOON HERALD" OFFICE.

Docks

It is a measure of the NBR's mercantile operations that, when the company lost its identity in the Grouping of 1923, it handed over whole, or partial, ownership of docks at Alloa, Bo'ness, Burntisland, Charlestown (Fife), Fisherrow (Musselburgh), Methil, Port Carlisle, Silloth, and Tayport Harbour. It had also invested in piers at Craigendoran, Mallaig, North and South Queensferry, and Tayport. In addition, the Rosyth Naval Dockyard was served by the NBR by a line built off the Inverkeithing-North Queensferry branch during the build up to the First World War.

Also served were the dock systems at Granton, Leith and Glasgow, the latter two of which were owned by independent organisations, known as Dock Commissions. The company did not send locomotives into Leith Docks until 1871 (four years after the Caledonian), and within six years the Leith Dock Commission felt it necessary to draw up guidelines for their use.

Now preserved in the National Archives of Scotland, the Leith Dock Commission guidelines are worth examining, as they draw attention to a facet of railroading which has practically vanished. These operating rules made clear that locomotive operations would be conducted 'only during the pleasure of the Commissioners', and the locomotives would have to be 'small and light'. Coke was the only fuel they could consume, and an 'iron grating' or other form of spark arrester had to be fitted. No train in and out of the docks could exceed 30 wagons, while 10 was the limit for trains travelling exclusively within the complex. These could not exceed a speed of 3 mph, except in the case of coal trains travelling between the hoists and the Seafield yards to the east, in which case 8 mph was permissable. Each train had to be accompanied by 'qualified engine pilots' wearing red caps.

The NBR's dock locomotives were, almost exclusively from the 1880s, Holmes's 0-4-0 saddle tanks, later classified by the LNER as Y9s, although Reid built a more powerful class of short-wheelbase 0-6-0s (later J88) in 1904. One of them distinguished itself with a dive into Kirkcaldy Harbour!

One of the heaviest of these maritime investments was at Methil, whose location so near to the mouth of the Firth of Forth, and so close to the mines of the Buckhaven area, made it an obvious port for exporting coal. The Wemyss family had put much investment into this port over the decades, but in 1913 the NBR developed the No. 3 dock there. In LNER days, there were 25 miles of track within the dock complex, although the coal trade later diminished, along with Fife's great reputation as a leading mining area. (The history of the complex is well described in Alan Brotchie's book on the Wemyss Private Railway). It was Methil which bore the brunt of one of Prince Philip's famous gaffes, when he described the town as 'a dump'. Hardly a fair comment on a hard-working community, with one of the most efficient coal-face-to-port operations to be found anywhere in the UK.

The 'one that got away' as far as dock installations were concerned, was Grangemouth, which fell into Caledonian ownership. This was careless of the North British, who placed their investment in Bo'ness instead. Posterity has decided that Grangemouth is now one of the two most important ports in Scotland, although admittedly much of its development has been fostered by the petrochemical industry, something which was almost unknown in North British days.

The End of the North British Railway

While the First World War ended in 1918 in victory for the United Kingdom and her allies, it brought about near-disaster for many of the country's railway companies.

All of them had found the logistical and manpower demands of the First World War to be almost insurmountable. To give an example in the case of the North British, the Rosyth-based Grand Fleet required the transporting of 14,000 men on leave, to home and back, over the 1918 Christmas period.

A couple of amalgamations resulted in England before 1920, but the most lasting effect of the war was that companies and their staffs became accustomed – as the civilian population did – to the effects of government control. Railway activities during the conflict had been co-ordinated, and to a considerable extent, controlled, through a new Ministry of Transport and its agency, the Railway Executive.

There was a general feeling that things could not go on as they had in the piping days of Edwardian peace. Nationalisation was an operational possibility, but the Labour movement was not yet strong enough to achieve what it later managed in 1948; the Liberal party had formed the government for some 12 years before the war, and its leader Lloyd George, called and won a 'khaki election' in December 1918. His Minister of Transport was an ambitious ex-North Eastern Railway official called Sir Eric Geddes, a strong supporter of centralising railway control. The result was a Railways Bill, drafted largely by him and introduced into parliament in 1921. It was to be the death-knell of the North British Railway, as well as all of the other companies, whether friend or foe.

The NBR was in a difficult position in relation to government control. As the largest Scottish rail concern, it had acted as the 'Secretary' Scottish company to the government during the war, and inevitably became involved in a number of administrative problems and conflicts. In particular, the Ministry was painfully slow in paying secretarial dues to the company, at a time when the latter badly needed new financial investment in permanent way and rolling stock.

Indeed, some English transport historians have alleged that the NBR all but ceased to introduce new locomotives after the war, leaving the 'Sassenachs' to deal with the problem of an ageing locomotive fleet. This ignores the fact that 'Scotts', 'Glens', and two new Atlantics were being introduced as the 1920s dawned – a considerable outlay for a cash-strapped company. The LNER's fairly prompt introduction of D1 and D11 4-4-0s on to former NBR metals after 1923 seems unnecessary in retrospect, although such 2-6-0 'alien' species as K2s and K3s probably represented a useful addition to the locomotive stud.

Despite the conflicts generated by its 'secretarial' status, the NBR accepted the principle of the 'Grouping' as it was called – the setting up of four super-companies from New Year's Day, 1923. While the Caledonian contested the way in which amalgamation was conducted, arguing that its stockholders were being short-changed, the North British Board was satisfied with the proposals, and accepted a resolution on December 22nd 1922 agreeing to give to their bankers 'authority to transfer all monies, deposits, bills of exchange, drafts, promissory notes, securities, and all other instruments of credit' to the new company, which soon was to assume the name of the London and North Eastern Railway.

The North British was to enter this east coast group as the second-largest company (after the North Eastern, in mileage terms) along with the Great Northern, Great Eastern, Great Central, Hull & Barnsley and Great North of Scotland. Of 26 proposed members of the new LNER Board of Directors, the NBR accepted an invitation to nominate four. The names forwarded were – William Whitelaw (NBR Chairman since 1918), and Messrs Gray, McCosh, and Murray. Of these, the new company was eventually to name a streamlined A4 Pacific after two (Whitelaw and Andrew K. McCosh), and less glamorous B1 4-6-0s after the other two (Murray of Elibank and Alexander Reith Gray).

In particular, the appointment of William Whitelaw as the Chairman of the new company was a massive compliment, both to him personally, and to the North British. Whitelaw had chaired the Highland Railway until 1912, and his tenure at the NBR earned him a reputation as a fair-minded individual with a good grasp of detail and unapproachable integrity (qualities not always found in company directors!).

Whitelaw's reputation had been enhanced during the run-up to the Grouping when the company was in conflict with the Ministry of Transport over a financial matter. The Minister, unbelievably, ordered the 'leaking' of correspondence between himself and the NBR chairman, something which simply didn't usually happen in those days, and which showed up Geddes as something less than a gentleman. After that, Whitelaw was a popular choice for the LNER chair!

The valediction Whitelaw received at the NBR's final AGM, on March 2nd 1923, was extraordinary, with his deputy chairman, the Duke of Buccleuch, telling the assembled stockholders 'he has been one whom we not only respect, but love'. This could almost be said of the company he led. History has remembered Whitelaw, (and his grandson, of the same Christian name, a minister in Conservative governments), while Sir Eric Geddes is unheard-of nowadays.

In contrast to the North British supplying the head of the new LNER company, the Caledonian Railway took no part in the formal establishment of the London Midland & Scottish Group, while stockholders fruitlessly challenged the amalgamation conditions. This resulted in the new group being racked by divisions between Crewe and Derby, an over-centralised administrative structure, and a ridiculous traction policy.

Their principal Scottish company made no contribution to the setting-up of what became Britain's biggest transport operation; the Scottish spirit, on the other hand, lived on in the LNER. The new company established three Areas, each with its own General Manager (the NB's James Calder was the first Scottish GM), and within eighteen months Edinburgh's own Sir Nigel Gresley was introducing a fleet of 40 Pacifics, half of them built in Glasgow, on to the East Coast route.

The final entry in the minute-book of the NBR Board of Directors summarises the last of their meetings, held on March 2nd 1923. It is a routine entry, simply listing approval of previous minutes and a report of business being prepared for the last Annual General Meeting, to be held later that day.

There was no ceremonial 'signing-off'. This most unglamorous of companies terminated its activities in the same no-nonsense businesslike way it ran its affairs during its 80 years of existence.

CHRONOLOGY

1843 NBR Prospectus issued.
1845 Edinburgh & Dalkeith taken over.
1846 Edinburgh-Berwick line opens.
1849 Edinburgh-Hawick line opens.
1862 Edinburgh Perth & Dundee Railway taken over.
1862 Waverley Route extended from Hawick to Carlisle and Hexham.
1865 Edinburgh & Glasgow Railway taken over.
1873 NBR introduces UK's first Sleeping Car.
1876 Anglo-Scottish services begin over Waverley Route and the Midland's Settle & Carlisle Route.
1878 Tay Bridge opens.
1879 Tay bridge collapses.
1883 Forth Bridge begins construction.
1886 Glasgow Union (Low Level) line opens.
1890 Forth Bridge opens.
1894 West Highland Railway opens to Fort William.
1895 Railway Race to Aberdeen.
1901 Railway Race to Edinburgh.
1901 West Highland Railway opens to Mallaig.
1906 'Atlantic' locomotives introduced.
1913 NBR opens Scotland's first Control Centre.
1914 First World War.
1922 NBR Chairman appointed head of new LNER.
1923 NBR absorbed into LNER.

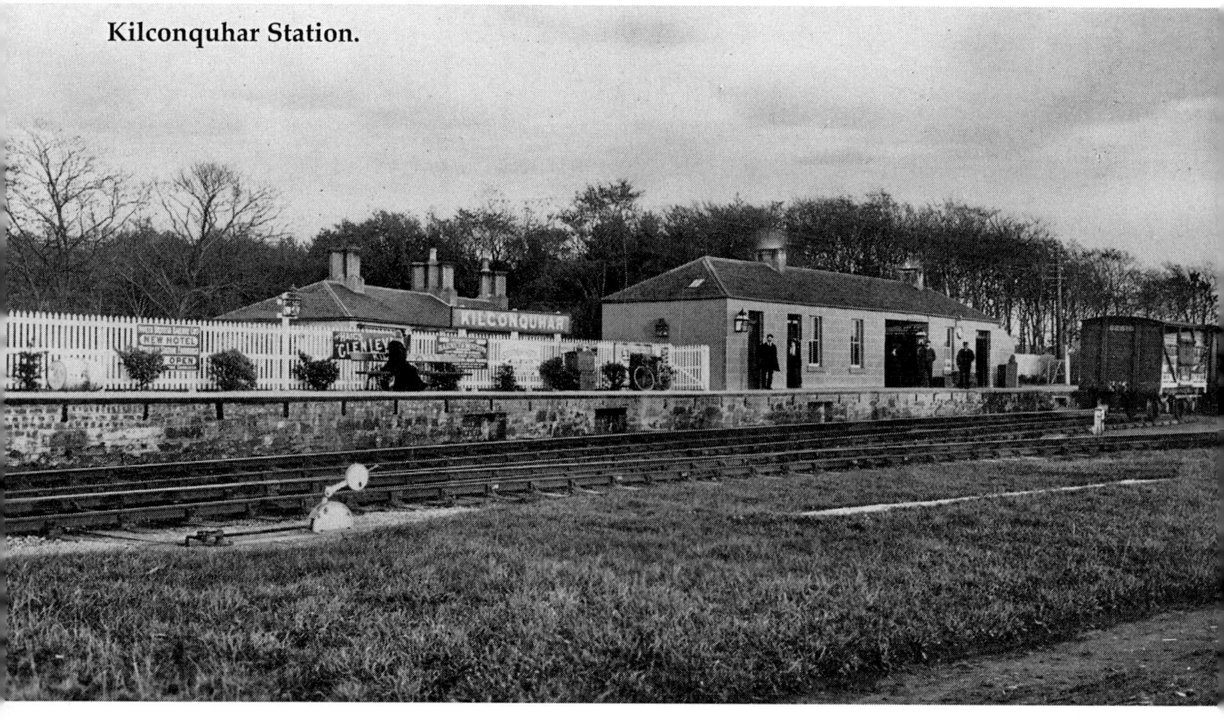

Kilconquhar Station.

Works Consulted

Primary records have been consulted whenever possible, including NBR company papers held in the West Search Room of the National Archives of Scotland at Charlotte Square, Edinburgh. These include board minutes from BR/NBR/1/1 onwards and miscellaneous documents in the BR/NBR/8 series. West Highland Railway minutes (BR/WEH/1 etc) and LNER documents have also been examined. The NAS staff are thanked for their helpfulness.

Secondary Sources:

Carter, Oliver. *An Illustrated History of British Railway Hotels 1838-1983*. Silver Link, 1990.

Deayton, Angus. *Steamers of the Clyde NBR and LNER*. Tempus Publishing, 2000.

Ellis, C. H. *The North British Railway*. Ian Allan, 1959.

Johnston, Colin and Hume, John R. *Glasgow Stations*. David & Charles, 1979.

Martin, D. and MacLean, A.A. *Edinburgh & Glasgow Railway Guidebook*. Strathkelvin Libraries, 1992.

Middlemass, T. *The 'Scottish' 4-4-0: its Place in Railway History*. Atlantic, 1994.

Mullay, A.J. *Rail Centres – Edinburgh*. Ian Allan, 1991.

Mullay, A.J. *Rails across the Border*. PSL, 1990.

Railway Correspondence and Travel Society. *Locomotives of the L.N.E.R.* Parts 3A, 4, & 5, 1979-1984.

Robertson, C.J.A. *The Origins of the Scottish Railway System 1722-1844*. John Donald, 1983.

Smith, W.A.C. and Anderson, P. *An Illustrated History of Glasgow's Railways*. Irwell, 1993.

Thomas, J. A *Regional History of the Railways of Great Britain. Vol. 6. The Lowlands and Borders.* (Revised by A.J.S. Paterson). David St. John Thomas, 1984.

Thomas, J. and Turnock, D. *A Regional History of the Railways of Great Britain. Vol.15. The North of Scotland. 2nd edition*. David St. John Thomas, 1993.

Thomas, J. *The West Highland Railway.* 3rd edition (with A.J.S. Paterson). David St. John Thomas, 1984.

Studies of the Berwickshire Railway and the Tweed Valley Railway, by A.J. Mullay and I.C. Coleford, appeared in *Railway Bylines Annual Number* 4 and *Summer Special* 6 respectively.

The author also wishes to record his thanks to the staffs of the National Library of Scotland and Edinburgh City Libraries.

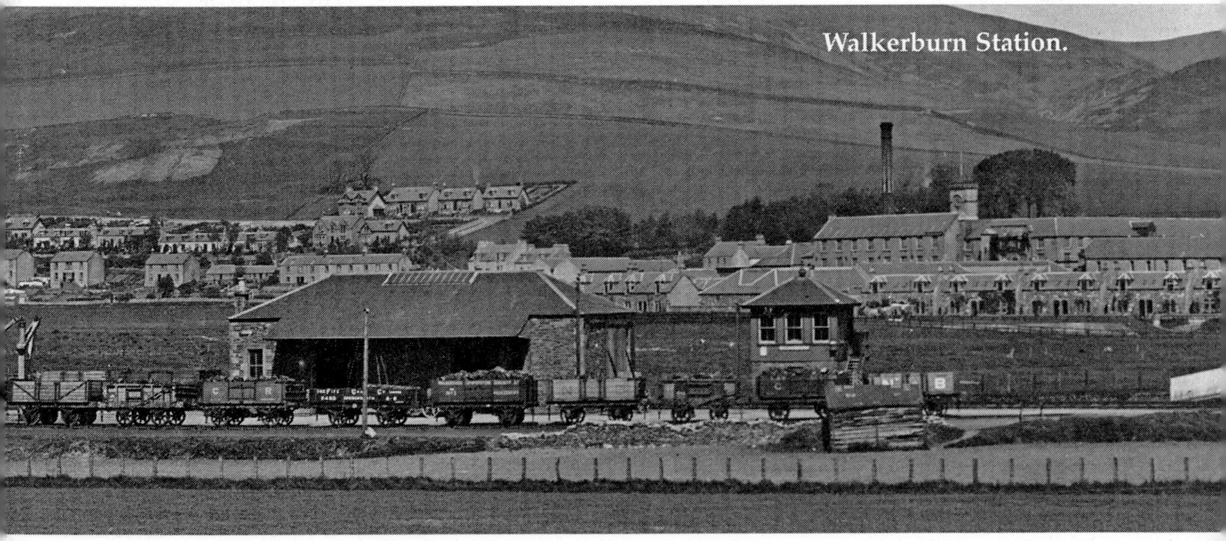
Walkerburn Station.

Summary of Information

Incorporated: November 1843.
First line opened (Edinburgh-Berwick): June 22nd 1846.
Principal amalgamations/takeovers: Edinburgh & Dalkeith (1845), Edinburgh Perth & Dundee (1862), Edinburgh & Glasgow(1865).
Absorbed into "Grouped" company (London & North Eastern Railway), January 1st 1923.
Size at Grouping = 1,389 route miles, 1,107 locomotives.
Principal workshops: St. Margaret's (Edinburgh) - 1865. Cowlairs (Glasgow) 1865-1923.
Most northernly point = Mallaig.
Most southernly point = Abbeytown, Cumberland.
Other interests: Union Canal, docks at Bo'ness and Methil, NB hotels in Edinburgh and Glasgow, Clyde and Loch Lomond cruising.
Principal Engineering features: Tay Bridge, Forth Bridge (consortium membership), Whitrope Tunnel, sub-Glasgow line.

Inverbervie the most north easterly point of the North British. The loading cranes of the goods yard on the far left are the only features of the station visible in this photograph. The shed on the far right marks the site of the turntable.

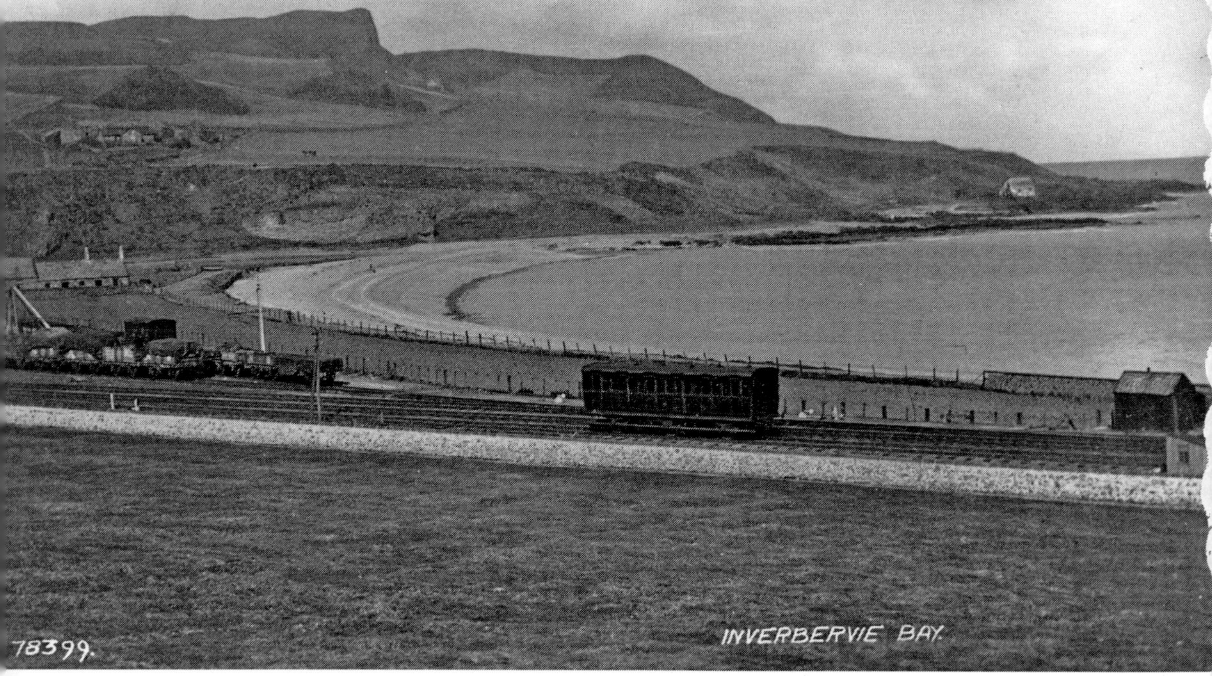